OLD KENT INNS

OLD KENT INNS

DONALD STUART

TEMPUS

Frontispiece: This is a print of the Tabard in South London in the eighteenth century. It is where many groups of pilgrims met up to start their journey to Canterbury and other Christian shrines throughout Kent.

First published 2006

Tempus Publishing Limited
The Mill, Brimscombe Port,
Stroud, Gloucestershire, GL5 2QG
www.tempus-publishing.com

© Donald Stuart, 2006

The right of Donald Stuart to be identified as the Author
of this work has been asserted in accordance with the
Copyrights, Designs and Patents Act 1988.

British Library Cataloguing in Publication Data.
A catalogue record for this book is available from the British Library.

ISBN 0 7524 3959 6

Typesetting and origination by Tempus Publishing Limited.
Printed in Great Britain.

CONTENTS

When you have lost your inns drown your empty selves.
For you will have lost the last of England.

Hillaire Belloc.

INTRODUCTION

Because there were so many Christians making their pilgrimages to Canterbury from both London and Winchester, a huge network of inns and alehouses was set up over the centuries. Queen Elizabeth I was responsible for many of the sixteenth-century inns to provide accommodation for the merchants and drovers who moved vast herds of animals about the county and into the capital.

There are still vestiges of ancient inns with large inglenook fireplaces, heavy oak beams, very low ceilings and even, on occasion, evidence of the old wattle and daub. Nearly all the old thatched roof inns have gone and the only one I came across was the Anchor Inn at Yalding. Often there are courtyards with a large side entrance that indicates they were coaching inns with stabling behind that have now been turned into beer gardens or car parking spaces. Some are still family run: in one case, the Red Lion at Snargate, for almost 100 years. This particular pub is on the CAMRA inventory of special pubs because it has not changed inside for almost 70 years. There has been a revolution in pub and inns over the past 25 years. Until only a few years ago, when pubs had limited hours by law dating from the First World War, they had to rely on local residents for business. In many farming areas of Kent much of the work has been taken over by vast combine harvesters and other machinery. This has led to the demise of the farm and estate workers on whom these inns relied.

Now most are open all day long and provide food of a high standard as they depend on motorists and other travellers for their business. This could not have been said once with some very basic inns with the outside toilets of yesteryear. If one were consider the typical inns of the seventeenth and eighteenth centuries, there would be few who would be prepared to stay, even overnight.

Kent provides a large number of historic inns in towns and villages, some of them with unusual architecture, furnishings, history, even the odd ghost or two. There are many well documented stories of haunted pubs and the most haunted village is said to be Pluckley. For many months I toured Kent by train and bicycle from Sheerness in the north to Dover in the south, and found a welcome at every inn.

Sadly there are many inns closing down for all sorts of reasons so, if a special trip is being made to a particular inn it would be advisable to telephone ahead. Occasionally pubs change names and this is where local Tourist Information Centres can help.

There is little doubt that there were bars or drinking houses set up throughout the country in Roman times and many of the pubs and inns of today may date from those times but there is little solid evidence for this. Pub is the shortened version of public house. In the past an inn meant a place to lodge travellers, pilgrims and horses; a tavern was a small drinking house which also supplied wine; and an alehouse was a drinking house where they sold beer, ale and cider but not wine. A brewhouse was a large building where they brewed their own beer. A tippler, or tapster, was a man or woman who ran an alehouse. These were sometimes nicknamed ale-drapers or beggar makers.

Although very few people actually look at inn signs, except to check they are at the right pub, they are a remarkable part of British social history. The first inn signs were bunches of actual vine leaves to indicate it was a pub and gave rise to the proverb 'A good wine needs no bush'. This was to indicate that there is no need to advertise a good wine or, indeed, anything else. The sign of the bush or vine goes back to Pompeii and Herculaneum.

In 1393 Richard II said, 'Whosoever shall brew ale in the town with the intention of selling it must hang out a sign, otherwise he shall forfeit his ale'. When a new ale was on offer an Ale Garland was hung outside the front door. This was to draw the attention of the Ale-Taster or All-Conner that a new brew was ready for examination. These officers of the crown were chosen each year at the Court Leet of each manor and if the ale fell below par the innkeeper was fined or ducked in the river. These officers would test ale by pouring some onto a bench and sitting there for 30 minutes and if their leather breeches stuck to the bench the ale was judged as being good.

Apart from the vine or a crooked billet (a bent piece of wood), the earliest forms of signs were pictures of such religious symbols as the cross, star and sun. Later signs would carry the arms of the local landowner, royalty or powerful nobles. Some inn signs are a piece of art in their own right and much imagination has gone into them.

For extra history details there are a large number of history and historical societies throughout Kent and a list of them can be obtained from Maidstone Library. For those with an interest in preserving historic inns there are a number of organisations they could support. These include CAMRA, the Pub History Society at PHS, 15, Hawthorn Road, Peterborough and the Inn Sign Society at 9, Denmead Road, Wednesfield, Wolverhampton WV11 2QS.

Donald Stuart
March 2006

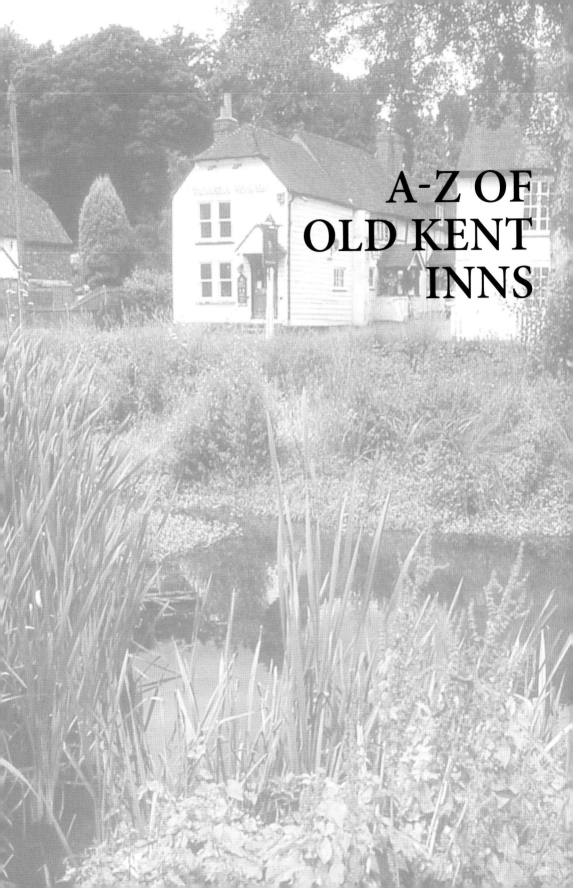

A-Z OF
OLD KENT
INNS

ACOL

In 1347 this was Acol, Saxon for oak trees. There is a famous chalk pit here called Smuggler's Leap. Riding Officer Anthony Gill pursued Smuggler Bill and both plunged into the pit during the horse chase. The bodies of two men were found, but only one horse; it is the missing one which is said to haunt the area on moonlit nights. During the Swing Riots of the 1830s many labourers left the area, paid for by parish councils, for the colonies in North America, New Zealand and Australia.

CROWN AND SCEPTRE

Opened as an inn in 1770 it was nicknamed the 'Clown and Spectre' after the landlord and landlady of that time. This was listed by Hogmanay in his *Etymology of the Bar*. The Crown and Sceptre is a two bar local with a collection of tie stubs from clubmen, regimental and old scholars, similar to the Bear at Oxford. The name 'bar', used in all inns and pubs, is from where drinks are dispensed and derives from 'bower', a small closet close to a porch at private houses, where drink was served. William Cobbett refers to this inn during his rural rides.

ADDINGTON

The farm of Eadda or Aedi, known as Edintone in 1086.

ANGEL

An ancient coaching inn that started here as an alehouse between 1350 and 1400 and stands on the village green. There is an interesting old staircase with corbels carved in the shapes of the Zodiac. Once it was a pilgrims' halt and has original beams and inglenook fireplaces. The inn has semi-Mansard roofs and a tall chimney. The Angel has been an inn name since the Middle Ages, showing the relationship between religious houses and travellers' hostels. It was also the Angel Noble, a gold coin minted in 1465 and surviving for three centuries.

ALDINGTON

The farm of Ealda and called Aldingtone by 1086. Aldington was the home of Elizabeth Barton, the Holy Maid of Kent, a servant girl with vision who foresaw plans of Henry VIII to divorce Queen Catherine and talked to people in authority. After confessing, she was executed and her head was put up on London Bridge. Richard Barham, writing in his *Ingoldsby Legends*, maintained that Aldington Frith was a meeting place for warlocks and 'other unholy subjects of Satan'.

BLACK RABBIT, ALDINGTON FRITH

A rare name for pubs and thought to be a corruption of rabbets; these were grooves on the edge or the face of wood or stone into which the end, or edge, of another piece is slotted. This would have been familiar to stonemasons and carpenters. The only other Black Rabbit I know is outside Arundel, Sussex. Just down the road from Aldington Frith is the White Rabbit at Bilsington. This is a large Victorian building on an earlier ale-house named after Lewis Carroll's white rabbit in *Alice in Wonderland*.

Walnut Tree,
Aldington

WALNUT TREE

Built in the reign of Richard II between 1377 and 1399 it was timber framed, wattle and daub with thatched roof until rebuilt. Inside the inn is a bread oven in an inglenook fireplace. The Walnut Tree was a beacon for local people and gives a twenty mile view of the coastline. Smugglers used it and a candle was put in the window when it was safe to bring in contraband goods. The infamous smuggler George Ransley married an Aldington girl, Elizabeth Bailey, whose family was also in the trade, and, before the Battle of Waterloo, ran this pub as a 'blind pig' or unlicensed. He bought brandy in France for 12s a gallon and sold it for £3 12s a gallon. There is still a spy-hole once used by the smugglers to view the marshes searching for Revenue men. Cockfighting took place here until 1904 and it is haunted by a man who was killed in the pub during a domestic quarrel and thrown down the well. There have also been reports of phantom children being seen and heard here. It is a large, corner, village pub with a number of bars and a restaurant with imitation firearms.

ALLHALLOWS-ON-SEA

Named after the twelfth century church Ho-all-hallows, when hoo meant spur of land. There have been rumours over the years that there is treasure buried in gardens once owned by Sir Harbottle Grimstone, a speaker at the House of Commons, who died in 1683. The village is noted for its savage north wind, known as the Boneless Wind, which may have been a corruption of the Roman navigators name for that wind, the *boreas*.

ROSE AND CROWN

A pub name found extensively throughout the country, it signifies loyalty to the monarch and has done since the seventeenth century. Once this inn was the meeting place for the hobelers, retainer soldiers with horses dedicated to protecting the seacoast at Yantlett and obtaining information about boats landing for the Pympes family and other wealthy estate owners. A boat was anchored off Yantlett Creek to protect against fishermen-smugglers.

APPLEDORE

Saxon Apuldor, the place where apple trees grow, and Apeldres by 1086. Once a busy shipbuilding town the Royal Military Canal was built here between 1804 and 1807 and was the most expensive military exercise of the time to keep out the Napoleonic troops. There was a fair at Appledore from a charter granted by Edward III until the end of the nineteenth century. Many of the houses around the inn are sixteenth and seventeenth century.

BLACK LION

Once called the Red Lion, this super village pub is similar in style and proportion to a town hall. There are black and white photographs and 200 unusual jugs on display. It is a Georgian brick-built building with a fine portico and a Norman-style parish church behind it. Inside the pub is a collection of flint and cock percussion firearms, brass blowlamps and antique furniture. Letters and parcels used to be left here for the landlord to distribute throughout the village. The black lion is usually a heraldic sign relating to Queen Phillipa of Hainault, the wife of Edward III. In Wales, it refers to Owain Glydwr and his father, Madoc ap Meredith, both of whom had black lions on their arms in the fourteenth century.

AYLESFORD

A ford belonging to a Saxon, Aegel. The village is the oldest continuously occupied place in England. There was a Bronze Age settlement and there is a magnificent fourteenth-century ragstone bridge.

LITTLE GEM

This little gem is between the village post office and a house and maintains it is the oldest and smallest pub in the county. The entrance is a lopsided door and even moderately tall people have to duck to get in. (One New Years Eve they got 200 people in for a party). The building went up in 1106 at the time of Henry I and was a shelter and hospice for monks and pilgrims; the first type of inn. For years afterwards it was occupied by farmers and, in 1630, the old wattle and daub was replaced by brick and tiles. It was galleried and then proper doors and windows put in.

Black Lion, Appledore

Aylesford Bridge

For some years, it was used as a shop before becoming an inn again. At a nearby Carmelite monastery, one monk was walled up for constantly breaking his vows. He is still seen walking up and down Monks Walk in the white tunic of his order.

CHEQUERS INN

A large half-timbered and white painted inn near what was the first river ford crossing on the River Medway. Because of this, many battles took place in and around the village over 1,500 years. The inn has bow-front windows, steeply pitched dormer windows and rooms with overhanging gables. Inside the fifteenth-century inn are low-ceilinged rooms with beams and large inglenook fireplaces. There is evidence that bullets from flintlock pistols are still buried in the walls dating from an English Civil War battle here in 1648.

BARNSOLE

BLACK PIG

A most uncommon name for a pub and may refer to the Gin Act of 1736 when landlords draped their inn signs with velvet or added 'black' to the pub name to show their disapproval or how they had gone into mourning. The name may also have come about from an expression, used since 1681, when 'to go pigs and whistle' meant to be ruined or made bankrupt. 'Black pig' also referred to Spanish galleons and there is history that part of the pub was built from timber brought ashore from the Spanish armada of 1588. The black pig was also a famous Kent breed of the animal. Barnsole was once a busy village when sheep and fleeces were on sale in the area.

Little Gem, Aylesford

Chequers Inn, Aylesford

The Black Pig, Barnsole

BEARSTED

In AD 695 this was Berghamstyde, homestead on a hill. The cricket pitch on the green is said to be the oldest in Kent and is surrounded by some fine old houses. The first game is said to have been played here in 1749. Baroness Orczy, authoress of *The Scarlet Pimpernel*, lived with her husband at a house in the village. (She used to travel around in her carriage and became really cross if local girls did not curtsey, or the boys doff their caps, as she went past). In 1830, John Dyke, aged 19, was hanged for hayrick burning but later found to have been innocent. An old Canadian cypress stump, known as the Mourning Tree, marks his grave and his was the last public hanging in the area.

OLD PLANTATION

A fifteenth-century inn that is perched above the village with a number of old oak beams inside. The open fire with iron dog-grate has some of the old stonework still surrounding it and a hunting horn above. The bars are a combination of old brick and upright timber beams with wooden floors. There are two stories about the pub name. One is that it was named for workers on a local wood plantation in Victorian times, the other that it was named after a man returning from the United States where he had owned sugar plantations.

WHITE HORSE

Opened early in the sixteenth century, the White Horse faces the fine cricket ground where a Civil War skirmish took place. The inn was used as a Commissary Court, for cases from Canterbury, and is black and white with gables. An old horse-mounting block has been converted to steps into one bar. In 1671 the landlord, Thomas Jemmett, had an inventory that included a hall, parlour, kitchen, dining room, coach house, five chambers, brew-house, a cellar with seven hogsheads of beer and £104; so he was a wealthy man. The poet, Edward Thomas, said of Bearsted, that one could hear the skylarks sing.

BECKENHAM

YE GEORGE INN

A raid on the pub by the local curate once found 12 men drinking there, including the Parish Beadle, when they should have been at church. Built in 1645 Ye George Inn is a large black and white building with weatherboarding and a fine portico. This is complemented by the extremely old black window shutters. Inside it is a large open bar with open fires. Above one open fireplace is a fine, etched mirror of Ye George Inn.

BENENDEN

In AD 993, this was Bingdene, a woodland pasture of Bionna.

KING WILLIAM IV

Benenden is a lovely unspoiled village with this sixteenth-century pub once used by the notorious Hawkhurst Gang of smugglers and cutthroats in the 1750s. There are two bars, one with an inglenook fire for the saloon bar, with low beamed ceilings and church pews; it was once a resting place for pilgrims. The inn was named after the Sailor King who went absent from the Royal Navy when he was only 23 but was rewarded by being created Duke of Clarence with £12,000 a year pension. One of his descendants, Princess Anne, went to Benenden School and, at one time, the pub landlord was Mr B. Tipples. Another famous resident of Benenden was Pretty Kitty Fisher, the one who found the pocket that Lucy Locket lost in the nursery rhyme.

Old Plantation, Bearsted

BENOVER

WOOLPACK

There really is a skeleton in the cupboard at this seventeenth-century inn. It used to be seated at the corner of the bar but this terrified some customers, so it was moved behind glass and now dwells below the dartboard. The building is over five hundred years old and has hanging hops and antique tools, antique firearms and beams in the bars. It is on three storeys with a steeply pitched cat-slide roof. The old timber framing has been exposed to provide partitions within the bars. Set back from the road this inn was once connected with the wool trade; that is clear from its name. It has a tile-hung frontage with the old stables behind and two bars. It was the headquarters of the Woolpack Gun Club. In 1757, a large eel was caught near here measuring 9ft 9in long, 18in round and weighing over 40lb. At one time, they let rooms at the Woolpack but the last man to book in was an escaped convict who was arrested there. A painting of this pub by Stanhope Formes in 1937 depicted this as the typical English country pub and many pubs still have that picture on their walls.

BICKLEY

CHEQUERS

Once a hideout of Dick Turpin this is an inn where curious sounds and happenings have occurred. Who is the ghost seen writing with a quill pen in a green velvet suit and plumed hat? Turpin was a dreadful man and, at this inn, he found the landlord had murdered his daughter and her lover so blackmailed him into using the pub as a hideaway and to keep his pistols. There are also tales of two women, dressed in eighteenth-century finery, who make an occasional appearance. It is set back off the road with a peg tile roof, half tile hung and white weatherboarded walls. Inside it is a warren of bars with low ceilings, and the timber-framing shows as partition walls. The Chequers is surrounded by 1920s-style 'Tudorbethan' houses.

BIDDENDEN

A Saxon called Bida had a woodland pasture here and the Siamese twins, Mary and Elizabeth Chulkhurst, were born here in 1100. They lived for 34 years, dying within six hours of each other. In their will, they left 20 acres of land called the Bread and Cheese lands that were used to supply food for the destitute. Each year this endowment provides a special biscuit for parishioners. It used to be bread, cheese, and ale until 1682 when the Rev. Giles Hinton, the rector, reported to Archbishop Sancroft, 'Even to this, the custom is with much disorder and indecency involved' and the ale was stopped. The oldest vineyard in Kent is on a 22 acre site outside the village

RED LION

In one bar of this village centre inn is a Tudor fireplace from 1586 and a beam with 1694 carved into it and a framed list of landlords over the years. It was probably opened by a soldier-archer on his return from Agincourt in 1415. The name is the most popular of all pub names, from the badge of John of Gaunt, fourth son of Edward III and father of Henry IV. Set opposite the village green the Red Lion has a cobbled front courtyard and many old beams, and large fireplaces are a main feature at this inn.

The Red Lion, Biddenden

THREE CHIMNEYS

There are rambling low-beamed bars in this black and cream fifteenth-century building that became a pub in the early 1800s. It opened, originally, to serve the local land labourers and hop-pickers. Once a half-timbered farmhouse dating from 1420, the pub was named the Three Chimneys when French prisoners of war were kept nearby. They gave their parole not to go further than the 'three ways' in the lanes, *les trois chemins* in French, which became, eventually, the inn name as the English heard it. There are a number of rooms that have been not been 'improved' for years with low beams, flagstones, wood panelling and log fires.

BIRLING

In AD 788, this was Boerlingas, the settlement of Baerla. The Rev. E.V. Bligh, vicar of Birling in the nineteenth century, concocted the Birling Cure for rabies. This included herbs and drugs in milk and sold in wine bottles at one guinea each. Then, sadly for the reverend, Louis Pasteur came on the scene and Bligh's cure disappeared.

NEVILL BULL

An open plan inn with red upholstered seats where cartoons of bulls abound along with beams and brass plate ware. It became the Nevill Bull in 1953 in memory of Michael Nevill, who was killed in the Second World War. This also commemorates the family name of Baron Abergavenny, Nevill, who arrived at Birling from Wales in the sixteenth century. The inn has an imposing white front with pitched and tiled roofs and massive chimneys. On the inn sign is a bull's head and two chained silver bulls for support.

Three chimneys, Biddenden

BOUGHTON LEES

FLYING HORSE

An imposing inn with unusually shaped windows and stone arches on both floors, it overlooks the village green. These windows are similar to the Dering windows at Pluckley. The flying horse is a reference to Pegasus, the winged horse ridden by Bellerophon in Greek mythology; the heraldic device of the Knights Templar; and the name of early stagecoaches. An old coaching inn from the fifteenth century, off the Pilgrims' Way, there are wooden beams and inglenook fireplaces. Recently a landlord found two freshwater wells below the pub and these are now covered with glass so that customers may see into them

BOUGHTON MONCHALSEA

The village name is a corruption of the surname of William de Montchensie, who died in 1287. His daughter, Dionysia, had the first French grammar book written in English, which is now in the British Museum.

COCK INN

Opened in 1604 by the Canterbury Diocese it was designed for pilgrims travelling from London. However, the roof construction suggests that the building went up in the thirteenth century. George III stayed here before inspecting 15,000 soldiers on nearby Cock's Heath. The name refers, sometimes, to cockfighting taking place there or where they sold cock-ale, a mixture of ale and the jelly of boiled fowl. In 1948, the film *Kind Hearts and Coronets* was filmed here with Alec Guinness and Valerie Hobson. The resident ghost is George, who hanged himself at the inn and spends the night knocking over chairs and throwing bottles of wine about. There is a brass memorial in the church to Thomas Evesham, a servant of Henry VIII, who died in the village in 1587, aged 101.

BRASTED

Originally Briestede, a broad place. A pleasant village green flanked by a row of Tudor-style cottages. Prince Louis, who became Napoleon III, trained his troops to re-conquer France in the parkland around here. A motley crew of 56 went to France to perform this task in 1840 but all were imprisoned.

WHITE HART

A fourteenth-century pub; during the Second World War, the aircrew from RAF Biggin Hill wrote their names on the blackout screens over the door. This has now been preserved behind glass in one of the bars. In fact, it is not the original one, which is now at Shoreham Museum, Kent. When the original board appeared on *The Antiques Roadshow*, it was described as priceless. There is timber framing that has now been opened up to show as partitions between bars and restaurants. Ruth Ellis, the last woman to be hanged, and the spies, Burgess and McLean, all dined here at different times. Opposite is a row of early eighteenth-century houses with small doors and wall hung tiling. A former landlady here, Katherine Preston, wrote of her time here with her husband in *Inn of the Few*.

BRIDGE

Old English *Bryge*, the place of the bridge.

PLOUGH AND HARROW

A three centuries old pub that was once a brewery, it is hung with hops and right at the centre of the community. This bucolic name for a pub has been in existence since the sixteenth century and sometimes can be found as the Plow. Often, when known just as the Plough, the inn sign shows the group of the seven stars in Ursa Major that are in the shape of a primitive plough. The landlord gives lessons in cellarmanship for other licensees and he is on the nude calendar of the pub book of the Millennium Year, 2000. Over 30 clubs run from here and once a month the local vicar works behind the bar. It also has a broadband connection and internet facilities.

WHITE HORSE INN

Once on the old London-Dover coach run this sixteenth-century inn is on the main street. It was not a full coaching inn but used for changing horses and for food, known as a baiting or halting house. Part of the inn was used as the blacksmith's forge so he could re-shoe any horses that had thrown their shoes along the badly made up roads. There are three main bars and a restaurant that has half-panelled oak walls. Over the large fireplace is an inscription from the English Civil War along with old firearms.

BROADSTAIRS

In 1914, the author John Buchan saw a wooden staircase down to the beach and called his classic thriller, *The Thirty Nine Steps*, after it. There is a Dickens museum in the original home of Mary Pearson, the inspiration for Betsy Trotwood in David Copperfield.

LORD NELSON

Regarded as England's greatest hero, the name Lord Nelson refers to Horatio Nelson, 1st Viscount Nelson, (1758-1805) and he has more inns named after him than any other person does. His greatest victory took place at Trafalgar, where the Royal Navy destroyed the combined French and Spanish fleets. Before that battle, he had hoisted his famous signal, 'England expects today that every man will do his duty.' Nelson had a complicated private life and was involved with Emma, Lady Hamilton, wife of the British envoy to Naples and by whom he had a daughter. This Lord Nelson is a short walk from Viking Bay and the harbour. It was licensed in 1815 to honour Lord Nelson whose body was on the *Victory* when it lay in Viking Bay for a few hours on its return from Trafalgar in December 1805. The ceiling is papered with Admiralty charts. It is opposite a newsagent's shop, the Victory News, and, on the outside walls of the pub, are painted large samples of knots including a sheepshank, rolling hitch, clove hitch, sheet bend and a bowline on a bight.

White Hart, Brasted

Neptune's Hall, Broadstairs

NEPTUNE'S HALL

Neptune was the Roman god of the seas and is the name of the eighth planet in the solar system discovered in 1846 by Catherine Herschel, the first British woman astronomer. Catherine's aunt, Caroline Hershel, worked with Sir William Herschel, (Caroline's brother), to discover the planet Uranus. The pub was used by the fishermen of the area and the interior was listed Grade II in 1999. There is some great panelling behind the bar and a large collection of bottled beers on display. Most of the bar has been opened up now although there is a very small Private Bar with an etched glass sign, a hangover from the 1930s. On the outside it is faux marble, clearly from the 1890s, and with a view down Harbour Street to the sea. Neptune's Hall opened originally in 1815 on the site of fishermen's cottages and was a hotel during the 1920s. It features in the CAMRA National Inventory of pub interiors of outstanding and historic interest.

TARTAR FRIGATE

An unusual pub name after a frigate in the Royal Navy. Tartar was a popular naval name and this particular frigate was the eighteenth in Royal Navy service. A Tartar was a native of Tartary that was, once, anywhere between the Crimea and the borders with China. They were a violent people, so any ship named Tartar would be imbued with ferocity in battle. This is a seventeenth-century inn with a flint frontage and is overshadowed by Dickens's Bleak House rising behind. The Tartar has bare wooden floors and pictures of old Broadstairs and boats. It is close to the sandy beach. There is an interesting etched glass door into the public bar and the fish restaurant above. The lifeboat station, opposite the pub, closed in 1912, after saving 275 lives since 1886, and is still well preserved.

Above: Tartar Frigate, Broadstairs

Right: The hudd at Brookland church

BROOKLAND

By 1262, this was Broklande, cultivated land by a brook. In 1821, there was a battle between the Aldington Gang of smugglers and the Revenue men in the village that became known as the Battle of Brookland, when Cephas Quested was the leader. He was captured at Brookland and later hanged at Newgate. Because of the frequency of such battles, the local doctor, Ralph Hougham, carried a special wallet for all his medicines and instruments for operating on the wounded. The Brookland clergy knew how to keep comfortable at funerals in wintertime; they had a hudd. This was a tall wooden box, similar to a sentry box, and they officiated from inside to keep their vestments and prayer book dry this whilst everyone else got wet. They still have a hudd at the church.

WOOLPACK

A fifteenth-century, timber-framed smuggling pub overlooking the dyke where all the beams are pegged without nails and there are wattle and daub remains with a cat-slide roof. In one bar is a spinning jenny that was used to divide the loot between the outlaws. This is a metal plate about nine inches square with an arrowed indicator. The Woolpack is a typical Kent house built in 1410 that was once a beacon keeper's cottage with low beams and old furniture. The inglenook fireplace is large enough to take a four-place table. There are still signs of a cellar tunnel that was used by the smugglers to escape and bring in contraband. Over the years, it has been used as a background for films about smugglers. There is a shove penny board in the bar marked for Georgian cartwheel pennies and a collection of water jugs above the bar.

Woolpack, Brookland

CANTERBURY

In 1859 Mr Wombwell, a menageries man, wanted to pull down Westgate to allow his elephants through; and nearly got away with it. The expression 'to canter' was from the Canterbury Gallop; monks and pilgrims making fairly fast and steady progress on horseback.

BISHOPS FINGER, ST DUNSTANS STREET

In the nineteenth century, many country signposts were made using a pointed finger. This became derisory slang for bishops who can point heavenwards but do not follow their own advice. One woman, Ellen Blean, housekeeper to such a canon, found he was having an affair with a younger woman. She poisoned them both with a meat pie and then disappeared. She was later found walled up at a house near this pub and every Friday night her ghost is said to wander this street. The black and white faced inn is only a few yards away from the imposing West Gate.

CHERRY TREE

A large corner inn that is said to be the oldest in the town because it is in a building dating back to 1372. Much of the present building is over 200 years old and was originally called the Fleur De Lis Tap. The latter part of that name meant it was an ordinary pub rather than the hotel of which it had been part. It is said to be haunted by Gilbert, a traveller who was beaten to death at the inn; five men were later hanged for his murder. He is said to be accompanied by a cat that rubs itself against customers' legs with faint mewing sounds. The inn sign has a different painting of a cherry tree on either side of the board. The original site was owned by Archbishop Thomas a Beckett in the twelfth century and Dickens stayed at this inn.

Bishop's Finger, Canterbury

Cherry Tree, Canterbury

Falstaff Hotel, Canterbury

EIGHT BELLS

There has been a pub on the site since 1798 but the current pub was rebuilt in 1902. Eight bells is the usual number of bells in a peal, and often the pub is near a church. When it is a harbour or seaside pub, it signifies the end of a watch. It is a red ceilinged pub with original embossed windows and some memorabilia from the First World War. There is also a piano and customers are encouraged to play for singalongs. It was once called the Three Queens when it was on the turnpike road as a coaching inn. There seems to be no reference to the meaning of the Three Queens as a pub name, so it may come from a card game.

FALSTAFF HOTEL

The Falstaff is the oldest hotel in the city, opening in 1403 and until 1783 known as the White Hart, a widely used pub name from 1377 and the heraldic symbol of Richard II. Westgate was closed at nightfall and pilgrims arriving after this had to be put up in inns outside the city gates. In the early 1900s it was known as Ye Olde Falstaff after the character that appears in three of Shakespeare's plays, playing the part of a bit of a lad and old rogue. In the early 1920s, it was of typical Tudor design with a high-pitched, tiled roof enclosing the second floor bedrooms and still had the leaded lights and casements of that period. According to an early authority of the early twentieth century, the interior had been 'tenderly dealt with' for even the inclusion of the modern kitchen, and all the trappings of the plumber's art, had been dealt with sympathetically.

Unicorn, Canterbury

MAIDENS HEAD

It has been an inn since the early seventeenth century with a timber frame and once had a brew house. The inn was called the Maiden and Princesses' Arms in 1619 and nicknamed the Head Maidens because the chief women of a Royal entourage to Canterbury stayed here. In 1692, it is recorded as billeting several soldiers.

YE OLDE BEVERLIE

This was once the home of the Parish Clerk, given to the church by Sir Roger Manwood. The clerk in 1692 was Will Sluce and he was the publican. It opened with a six day licence and was later associated with the Kent Cricket Club. It is a well-known centre for the game of Bat and Trap that was invented here. In 1838, it was known as the Beverly Arms.

UNICORN AT ST DUNSTANS

This was a dwelling house in the sixteenth century when it was owned by a draper, Robert Budden. In the early seventeenth century, 1604, an alehouse licence was granted. It earned a reputation as a bawdy house for some years. The unicorn is a beast of legend with a horse's body and a single long horn on its forehead. It was thought to possess magical properties and a unicorn was the name for a Scottish gold coin in the fifteenth and sixteenth centuries. The name was also used for the formation of three horses pulling a carriage with one lead horse and a pair. This inn has low beams and ceilings around an island bar and is close to the railway station.

CAPEL-LE-FERNE

From the Middle English, *chapel*, and known in 1377 as Capel ate Verne, by the ferny place.

VALIANT SAILOR

This sort of name was popular just after the English Civil War, appealing to soldiers and sailors who returned home and took pubs. This Valiant Sailor was used by coaches and travellers and one landlord painted the Latin *Siste viator* on the wall meaning 'stop and rest travellers'. There is also a story that it was given its name because of the constant battles between the fishermen of the area and Dover and the local men would retire here to regroup. Near here is Steddy Hole where, in 1855, there was a murder most foul when a Serbian soldier, Dedea Remanixies, serving with the British Army, killed an 18 year old girl and her sister. Following his trial at Maidstone he was hanged before a crowd of 5,000.

CHALLOCK

In AD 824, this was known as Cealfalocum, an enclosure for calves. The village also claims to have been the birthplace of William Caxton, the father of English printing.

CHEQUERS

Right on the village green the Chequers has been here for three centuries. It is one of the un-modernised pubs with low beams, walls of brick and plaster, an inglenook fireplace and a well-stocked bookshelf. There are several reasons for the name Chequer, or Chequers, for a pub. One is that is that of a board game originally found at Pompeii; the second is that it was used as a board for counting money or taxes that gave rise to exchequer; and thirdly that (in some areas) of Kent it was the fruit of a wild service tree or shadbush that was used to sweeten beer.

CHARING

In AD 799, this was Ciorrincg, either a bend in the road or Ceorra's place. In 1935, a quantity of gold and silver was found in the Charing Hills but not enough to make mining worthwhile. Charing once had the engineering works where Alf Cackett made penny-farthing bikes and built the first diamond-framed bicycle in Kent. It is almost a 1930s-style village with a butcher and baker, a fishmonger, a licensed grocer and a watchmaker. In 1590, there was a dreadful fire at the church of St Peter and St Paul caused by a man with a shotgun setting fire to the wooden shingle. It is said that it was then that the relic of the block on which John the Baptist had been beheaded was also burnt. This block was maintained to have been brought back by King Richard the Lionheart from the Holy Land. Next door is the old palace that was visited by Henry VII in 1507 and Henry VIII in 1520 and 1544, who received it as a gift from Archbishop Cranmer in 1545. In 1629, it was bought by Charles I and is now a private residence.

BOWL INN

An unusual name for a pub and refers to a large punch bowl that was once held in the village. When there was national rejoicing the bowl would be filled with ale and ladled out to everyone in the village. A Bowl pub in London was named after the bowl of ale handed to prisoners on their way to be hanged; the expression 'on the wagon' comes from this occasion. Several guards accompanied the prisoners into the pub for their last drink while one would remain on guard;

on the wagon. At the top of the North Kent Downs, the Bowl Inn is sixteenth century and has a large garden including camping facilities.

CHARTHAM

ARTICHOKE INN

This vegetable was introduced to England in the early sixteenth century from Italy and several inns throughout the country are named after it. Because of its distinctive shape, it was useful as a sign for seedsmen, gardeners and innkeepers. (The Queen's Head and Artichoke in London was named after the widow of Louis XII of France, who was fond of artichokes, and her gardener named his tavern after this.) Surrounded by eighteenth-century cottages and an attractive Gothic church, this Artichoke Inn is fourteenth century and the original details came to light during renovation work in 1994 when old timbers were exposed. There are two inglenook log-burning fireplaces and original medieval windows with a collection of drinking jugs.

CHART SUTTON

When land was granted here by Coenwulf, King of Mercia in AD 814 it was described as open land with a small Saxon church. The village was almost wiped out by the Black Death and, in the mid-nineteenth century, it almost died again when so many villagers escaped to Canada because of rural starvation.

LORD RAGLAN

Raglan was a military general who served in the Peninsular War as military secretary to the Duke of Wellington. He was Commander-in-Chief of the British troops in the Crimea in 1854 and thought to be one of the most ineffective military leaders ever. The Lord Raglan is originally seventeenth century and there are super views across the orchards. Inside are old beams, open log fires and a huge array of hanging hops. Outside it is white painted brick with white weatherboarding and an ancient hand plough and seeder. Inside the bucolic nostalgia is carried on with a large milk churn that was once used to collect milk from the farms. It has been said the inn is haunted by 'Flasker' Beasley, a farmer cum smuggler and a member of the Hawkhurst Gang, who lived nearby.

CHATHAM

TRAFALGAR ARMS

On a hillside, out of town, the inn is named after one of the women said to have fought at Trafalgar on the frigate Euryalus, who had lived at the New Inn, Chatham. The New Inn was badly damaged in bombing raids in the Second World War and, when rebuilt, it became the Trafalgar Maid. This was after Jane Townshend who was at the Battle of Trafalgar on 21 October 1805. It is not clear if she fought here dressed as a man, was a nurse or was even one of the women smuggled aboard by some officers, or a prostitute below decks. This was not uncommon and, in 1815, when a ship's captain called for all hands to fight a fire, five women appeared. A pimp working out of Chatham, a pub landlord called 'Nasty Face', provided girls at three shillings a time and they sailed with the crew. A 'son of a gun' was a bastard born to these women, having been conceived close to such armaments. There are records of several women serving as sailors. One of them was Mary Lacy,

Trafalgar Arms, Chatham

who ran away from domestic service in Kent and wrote an autobiography under her male name of William Chandler about her time as a ship's carpenter. In 1771, she received a pension from the Admiralty. Another woman sailed as 'William Brown', again out of Chatham, and all was revealed when she had to be flogged and stripped to the waist. The Trafalgar Arms is a large pub on an estate where there was Victorian terraces housing the men who worked in the dockyard.

CHIDDINGSTONE

Known as Cidingstane in 1110 it was a stone connected with a Saxon man Cidd or Cidda and there is a legal document referring to the piece of land in AD 814 in a grant to the Archbishop of Canterbury. Hidden up a nearby lane is the Chiding Stone that is said to have been a Saxon boundary; a Druidical altar; a place where neighbours would sort out their problems and be 'chided' or where husbands took their errant wives to be flogged. The stone is also said to have been used by travelling preachers.

Castle Inn, Chiddingstone

CASTLE INN

In the shadow of the parish church, the Castle has a nineteenth-century façade hiding a seventeenth-century interior. The building dates back to 1420 when it was the Waterslip House and first used as an inn by the Weller brothers in 1712. It was first licensed in 1730 when the seed drill was invented by Jethro Tull. The completely Tudor village was bought by the National Trust in 1939 for £25,000. The pub is tile hung with casement and mullion windows and one bar is called 'The Confessional'. (Is this because it is directly opposite the church?). The Castle Inn is heavily beamed and the whole area is said to be the finest street in Kent. In the rear garden is a pool with a fountain and benches for al fresco drinking. There is a myriad of bars, including a traditional public bar with barrels used as tables and seats, an inglenook fireplace and a collection of books for the contemplative drinker.

CHILHAM

Three origins have been given for this village name: the farm of a Saxon man called Cilla; a woman called Cille or, perhaps, Old English *cille*, a spring. The castle site is where, in 55BC, the local Britons gathered to fight off the Roman invasion. There is a heronry at the castle and it is bad news if the herons do not arrive by St Valentine's Day, as this forecasts doom for the family.

WHITE HORSE

The white horse is the emblem of Kent and has been popular as a pub name since the Hanoverians. This White Horse was built as a thatched farmhouse in 1422. It eventually became an alehouse and used by the church behind it for festivals, weddings and funerals. Half a century ago, two skeletons were found at this elegant pub on the square and, according to forensic evidence, to have been soldiers from Wat Tyler's revolutionary army killed at the Battle of Chilham in 1381. Again, during renovation, a huge inglenook fireplace was uncovered with a Lancastrian Rose carved onto the mantel-beam. In one bar is a collection of hand bells and outside is a walled garden with cherry trees. An elderly gentleman, in clerical garb, is seen standing at the fireplace with his hands clasped behind his back at ten o'clock each morning. A former vicar is said to have committed suicide here, many years ago, and comes back to haunt the pub.

WOOLPACK

The pink-washed Woolpack was built in 1422 and has tenancy records going back to 1428 as Joan of Arc took Orleans. The woolpack or woolsack was the same item that was prepared for sale or delivery. The woolpack had a weight of 240 pounds but a woolsack was of indeterminate weight. Now it is the seat of the Chancellor, who sits on the Woolsack in the House of Lords as a reminder of how much the national wealth depended on that. Legend has it that a tunnel once connected this inn with Chilham Castle and was wide enough for a coach and horses to drive through to carry prisoners who had been tried at the inn when it was a courthouse. The Woolpack is haunted by a Grey Lady who appears regularly in the front bedroom and who stands beside the fireplace. Once there was a workhouse next door for the poor and homeless.

CHILLENDEN

In AD 833, this was Ciollandene, the valley of Ciolla.

GRIFFIN'S HEAD

Dating back to 1286 when the first justices of the peace were installed in England, the building is a black and white timbered Wealden hall house that was once a farmhouse. It was a monks' hospice until the Dissolution of the Monasteries in 1536. A griffin was a fabulous monster said to be the offspring of the lion and the eagle; thus the noblest animal of all. The Griffin's Head is a rambling, heavily beamed inn with flagstone floors, two inglenook fireplaces, old photographs and oil-pressure lamps. It began as an alehouse for locals in 1743. In 1776, it took a full licence as a coaching inn on the Deal to Canterbury run. There is still evidence of the old wattle and daub walls inside. Once a month there is a meeting of classic car collectors and their prized possessions.

COBHAM

Cobba hammes mearce, in AD 993, it was the enclosure of a man called Cobba. One Lord Darnley (of Cobham) was a famous cricketer who played for Kent from 1877 to 1883. In 1882 England lost to Australia in a test match and the *Sporting Life* issued an obituary that cricket had died as a game and would be cremated and taken back to Australia. In a following tour of Australia some local women there collected the burned ashes of a cricket bail, put them in a pottery urn and gave it to English captain; thus was born the Ashes.

Griffin's Head,
Chillenden

LEATHER BOTTLE

An old beamed pub used by Dickens in the *Pickwick Papers* and opened in 1628 as the Massachusetts Bay Company was granted territory there by Charles I. The inn was also a Royalist meeting place during the Civil Wars. On the walls in stone-flagged corridors are many old Dickensian prints. Cobham was on the London to Dover stagecoach run and this was one of the main inns. Although the pub name is not uncommon, this one was named when a leather bottle was found with a bag of gold sovereigns alongside an old cannon ball from an ancient battle.

DARNLEY ARMS

Said to have been built in the twelfth century (which makes it the oldest secular building in Cobham), with a tunnel to the church used by smugglers hiding their booty in the eighteenth century. Named after the earls of Darnley, I like to think it was named after the Lord Darnley, second husband of Mary, Queen of Scots, who had him taken to a lonely house outside Edinburgh where the house, and Darnley, were blown up by gunpowder by the Earl of Bothwell in 1567. The inn is haunted by the fifteenth-century Sir Thomas Kemp, who spent his last night here before execution.

CONYER

The area was once infamous for the North Kent smugglers. After some dreadful battles, they were finally put to flight by a leading Bow Street Runner, one James Bond.

SHIP AND SMUGGLER INN

Since it was built in 1642 the Ship has had a chequered career as a private house, a blacksmith's shop, a bakery and then as an alehouse. Overlooking the creek and marshland it maintains a nautical air with fishing nets hanging from the ceilings, seagoing charts, maps and other nautical ephemera including a captain's chair. In one of the battles, between the smugglers and the Bow Street Runners, near the Ship some of those captured were hanged or transported. One convict, who did return from the colonies, was drowned in a storm just outside this pub. He is said to be the gentleman dressed as a seafarer who still haunts it.

Leather Bottle, Cobham

COOLING

Old English Culingas in AD 808, a settlement of Cul or Cula. In the local graveyard is a series of tombstones said to have inspired Charles Dickens for *Great Expectations*. There are 13 lozenge shaped chest stones marking the eighteenth-century graves of the Comport children, none living more than 17 months, being killed off by malaria, then a virulent local disease. There were also local smugglers who hid their goods in the church pulpit. Sir John Oldcastle, who owned the manor after 1408, believed that church wealth should be shared out with the poor. This upset the Archbishop of Canterbury and Sir John escaped arrest but was eventually caught in London and hanged in 1417. He is said to have been the source of Shakespeare's Falstaff.

HORSESHOE AND CASTLE

Once called the Castle it caught fire in the First World War and there was not enough water in the village pond to put it out, so it was re-built. It now has a distinct 1920s feel to it with overhanging and beamed rooms and inside is an island bar serving several rooms. Outside there is a curious truck or passenger-carrying wagon that may have been an agricultural vehicle to take four workers to the field, and a 1920s style advertising model.

Lozenge graves, Cooling

Horseshoe and Castle, Cooling

CUDHAM

The village of a Saxon man, Cudda, and with a view across the Kent countryside to envy.

BLACKSMITHS ARMS

In 1638, this was a farmhouse with stables and a blacksmith set up business here and, by 1729, it was both a smithy and alehouse. In 1730, it became an inn and an original iron anvil still stands outside. One landlord's son, Harry Relph, who was his sixteenth child born in the inn, later became 'Little Titch' in the music hall. A pair of his 28in-long stage shoes and other props are now in the pub behind glass. High on the pub front is a blue plaque erected by Bromley Council. Little Titch, who was born in 1867 and died in 1928, was only 4ft 6in tall with six digits on each hand. The beer garden is the most elegant and colourful that I have found in Kent, large and tree shaded. They have their own gardening team to keep it in trim; and a most winsome sight it is.

Blacksmith's Arms, Cudham

Huffler's Arms, Dartford

Wat Tyler, Dartford

DARTFORD

The Queen's jeweller, Sir John Spielman was granted a licence to set up the first paper mill in England in 1586 and brought the first two lime trees to Kent in 1607. His wife had a court jester's hat on her coat of arms and Spielman used it as watermark that may have given rise to 'foolscap', now fullscap, or A4 size paper.

HUFFLERS' ARMS

Now a unique pub name after the boatmen who ferried goods from the ships' chandlers out to the ships anchored offshore. They were an unlicensed group and also known as 'hobblers' or 'hovellers' suggesting they may have lived in crude hovels along the river bank. There is a huffler's pole hanging from the ceiling above the bar. This pole is like a pikestaff with spear point and hook. On the pub walls are ships' wheels and horse brasses. There was a Hovellers' Boat Inn at Dover and, in 1840, a boy, Richard Doyle, was caught collecting horse manure outside the pub and was fined fourteen shillings. He had previously been jailed for this offence. At Ramsgate there was a Hovelling Boat Inn that closed in 1909 and was named after the men who rowed out to the treacherous Goodwin Sands to rescue wrecked sailors before the lifeboat system was set up.

WAT TYLER

A town centre pub that was once lived in by Wat Tyler, who led the Peasants' Revolt of 1381 along with Jack Straw and John Ball. It is a long narrow pub said to have opened in the fourteenth century. Once known as the Crown and Anchor there is now, on the inn sign, a painting of the dagger that slew Tyler. There is a potted history on the outside wall and the long bar leads to a raised dais. The interior walls were timber framed and are now stripped back to feature as room dividers.

DEAL

Addelam in 1086 and Dela by 1158, a hollow or valley. Julius Caesar beached his boats here after being beaten back at Dover. A Deal man, William Jarman, aged 19, was the first man to row solo across the channel to France in 1911.

ADMIRAL KEPPEL, MANOR ROAD

Viscount Keppel commanded the British fleet at Ushant in 1778 and won several sea battles against the French. As a young midshipman, he was with Admiral Lord Anson on a round-the-world voyage between 1740 and 1744. Keppel was a forebear of Alice Keppel, mistress of Edward VII and great-grandmother of Camilla, the wife of Prince Charles. The Admiral Keppel is a fine inn opposite the parish church with one long bar made up of several previous small bars. Although modernised it still has white ceilings with black beams. A copy of the painting, by Reynolds in 1780, hangs in the bar and is also on the inn sign. Included in the nautical ephemera is a poster claiming Britannia Triumphant after the Battle of Trafalgar in 1805 when Lord Nelson was killed in battle. It is a two-storey, cream painted building and the beer garden is shaded by a large tree.

KING'S HEAD, BEACH STREET

There is a warren of bars here with so much in the way of pub decoration it is difficult to take it all in. There are tankards hanging from the ceiling, framed fishermen's knots, a collection of miniature and full size cricket bats, a poster from 1805 praising the Old British Tars for what they had just accomplished, ships wheels, brasses and badges. It is named after George III and there is a picture of him in 1764 in the bar and a similar one on the inn sign. It has good views of passing ships and one that appears once every 50 years in full sail is the phantom *Lady Lovibond of Deal*, lost 13 February 1724 with 50 lives. When the Captain took his bride on board the sailors all muttered 'Bad Luck.' She had been the girlfriend of the first mate and, driven mad with jealousy, the mate deliberately rammed the ship into the Goodwin Sands.

SHIP, MIDDLE STREET

An old fashioned two bar pub, the Ship is in the conservation area of Deal where they often hold historical re-enactments. (Strangers beware; these re-enactments can be quite spontaneous). There are wooden floors throughout the inn and Royal Navy cap ribbons hang on the walls and ceilings. It has not been got at by the modernisers and is left with a small back room and a piano in the other bar and is free of jukeboxes and gaming machines. This is another of the treasures of Deal, with a VR postbox on a nearby house wall and one house, an ordinary Regency cottage, called Christmas House.

DENTON

The parish churchyard here is said to have inspired Thomas Gray (1716-71) to write his famous *Elegy in a Country Churchyard*. Gray was a frequent visitor to the village. (However, this is also claimed by a parish church at Stoke Poges, Buckinghamshire). It is not easy to find the entrance to the churchyard; it is about 200 yards west of the Jackdaw on the left hand side of the road with a lodge beside it. Carry on about 200 yards up this lane passing a group of trees. There is a long metal fence running beside the road on the right hand side with a kissing gate. Go through this and cross the field on a pathway into the copse of trees. Denton Court, next to the church, was the home at one time of Mary Stephen-Smith, author and short story writer, who was one

Admiral Keppel, Deal

Denton Graveyard, Denton

41

Jackdaw Inn,
Denton

of the models for the most famous of all Victorian paintings, *And when did you last see your father.* She was the niece of the painter, William Yeames, who executed that picture in 1878 and her brother, James, was the model for the boy being questioned.

JACKDAW INN

A local resident of Denton was the Revd Richard Harris Barham, author of the *Ingoldsby Legends*, one time vicar of Warehorne and Snargate. The Jackdaw was the Red Lion until renamed in 1969. This was after the famous poem *Jackdaw of Rheims*, about such a bird that stole the Cardinal-Archbishop's ring. The building went up in 1645 and later became an alehouse before becoming a coaching inn. The premises were built by Thomas Leythorpe, Gentleman of Elham, in 1645 as a farmhouse and were licensed as an inn in 1756 to Andrew Snell. On the inn sign there was a painting of the Bell Harry Tower at Canterbury Cathedral but this has been replaced by an impressive jackdaw with wings outspread.

DODDINGTON

The farm of Dudda or Dodda. Local tradition has Richard the Lionheart stopping at Doddington when returning from the Crusades. He is said to have been carrying the block on which John the Baptist was beheaded and, in 1467, the church dedicated the church to the Beheading of St John the Baptist because it had passed through the village. There is a monument here to George Swift, a law student, who died in 1732 'By an Unfortunate Fall from a Chariot'.

CHEQUERS

Originally twelfth century it has played a large part in the history of Doddington. It was used by pilgrims going to and from Canterbury and was a place where taxes were collected. The large apartment in the roof is where the post-boys and postillions slept and their passengers in rooms below. The same part of the upper rooms were used as a 'smugglers' dump'. There are two main bars with a stable door entrance, one fourteenth century and the other fifteenth, that were once four bars, one for each of the social classes. There are fine mullion windows, inglenook fireplaces and a 'secret' room used as a priest hole at the time of the Reformation. The Chequers is also one of the famous haunted pubs of Kent; it is haunted by a Cavalier who was killed in an upstairs room and is said to be seen peering through an overhanging window. There is also the ghost of a woman, the wife of a previous landlord, heard playing the piano in the private quarters. It is also bang up to date with a satellite broadband and wireless internet for the village.

DOVER

One of the original Cinque Ports, Dover is a main port between southern England and the continent. It was known as Dubris in the fourth century, Dofras by AD 700 and Dovere in the Domesday Book of 1086. It was named after the stream here, called the Dour, a Celtic river name.

Chequers, Doddington

Golden Lion, Dover

ADMIRAL HARVEY, BRIDGE STREET

This typically late Victorian design pub is on the site of a previous one and named after Sir Eliab Harvey (1758-1830) a descendant of the anatomist, William Harvey, who discovered the circulation of blood. Sir Eliab commanded the *Fighting Temeraire* at Trafalgar and was made admiral in that year, 1805. It opened in 1829 as an alehouse and was licensed in 1857 when Mr Clare was landlord who also sold dairy produce. The annual fair was held in the area but the pub became so boisterous Mr Clare was shown the yellow card by the magistrates. When rebuilt in 1905 it cost £1,000 to do so. It was shaken up a bit when a bomb landed in the back yard in 1917.

GOLDEN LION, PRIORY STREET

A one bar corner pub with pictures of the local Winkle Club, named after Pickwick's friend, which raises money for local charities and old photos of the pub itself along with maritime prints. It was once two cottages and opened as an inn in 1846, at the same time that the *Book of Nonsense* was published by Edward Lear, and they advertised good stabling. At one point, they had a 5 a.m. licence for early morning passengers leaving for the continent. There had been an earlier Golden Lyon that opened in 1736 on a nearby site almost in the shadow of Dover Castle. The present pub is known locally as the Golden Roarer.

Sir John Falstaff, Dover

SIR JOHN FALSTAFF, LADYWELL

As this flamboyant pub opened in 1869, the Suez Canal was being opened to shipping. The Sir John appears to have undergone a Gothic revival about the early 1890s when pub designers dispensed with the old Tudor and Elizabethan look and went in for lots of marble, mirrors, etched glass and mahogany fittings. In 1934, the local council tried to make a land-grab for the site to build a police station, but, somehow, this was foiled. A bit of a Bobby Dazzler, this pub; but one to be cherished. Falstaff appears in three of Shakespeare's plays, described as a huge fat man, a boasting liar, who makes out to be a loveable rascal. Some philologists have found a play on Shakespeare's name, 'false-staff'.

WHITE HORSE, HUBERT PLACE

In 1778, the 25th Foot Regiment, the Edinburgh Regiment, was in the garrison and this pub named City of Edinburgh after that occasion, although there is another legend that it was named the City of Edinburgh after a wrecked freighter of that name in the Dover Straits when they used the nameplate off the ship. It was renamed the White Horse in 1818, after the Kent emblem, and was used to hold inquests during the early 1800s. After one such inquest on a sailor washed ashore, there have been stories of a man in uniform playing a tin whistle and haunting one of the bars. The original building went up during the reign of Edward III in 1365 when it was occupied by the verger of St James's Church, next door. By 1574, it had been taken over by the Ale Taster for Dover.

DUNKS GREEN

KENTISH RIFLEMAN

Here is an ancient village pub with beams and a Tudor inglenook fireplace. The inn sign is famous as it shows a member of the Home Guard during the Second World War. A stream flows below the cellars and, at one time, the doors here into the public bar were only four feet high, not much taller now. For some curious reason it was nicknamed the 'Raffish Gentleman'. Built early in the sixteenth century the very low-beamed public bar has a collection of ancient firearms.

DYMCHURCH

Deman circe in 1100, meaning the church of the judge. The Jurats of the Level of Romney Marsh were created and allowed to govern themselves provided they maintained the sea walls. In the late 1200s smuggling wool, or owling, began when Edward I set a tax on exported wool. This lasted up to 1724 when the French found they could get cheaper wool in Ireland.

SHIP INN

Another old smuggling pub that appears in Russell Thorndyke's books, *Doctor Syn* and *Doctor Syn Returns*, as he lived in this area for many years. Above the door of this inn is an unusual carved and gilded sailing ship on the high seas. The Ship Inn is low beamed with an attractive staircase. In 1787, the Dymchurch Gang exported some live sheep to France but they were caught as they returned and were jailed. The landlord of the Ship passed an iron crowbar through the window of the jail so they could break out. One room at the Ship has an iron ceiling from when the Wealden ironworks were still working in the eighteenth century.

EAST PECKHAM

BUSH, BLACKBIRD AND THRUSH

This strangely named pub is cottage style with log fires. Once it was two, tile-hung fifteenth-century farmhouses and has oak beams and sloping floors. The roof is a 'catslide' with one roof covering two floors. The pub was originally called the Fountain. This traditionally built pub has two bars that are separated by a large brick fireplace. The bush was used to denote the Roman *tabernae* when they built roadside wine houses during their occupation; but the blackbird and thrush is anybody's guess. To students of 1970s ephemera they still use Oranjeboom lager ashtrays.

EASTRY

In the ninth century, this was known as Eastoreg, the eastern district or region. At the end of the nineteenth century there were people living in the village who claimed to have walked ten miles to Canterbury through the seventeenth-century chalk mines. It is legend that Archbishop Thomas a Becket hid in those caves when he was waiting to escape from England through Sandwich or Deal in 1164.

Bush, Blackbird and
Thrush, East Peckham

BULL INN

A sixteenth-century coaching inn with outside stabling, the Bull once had a black and white frontage. Now it is a flat faced inn with large windows overlooking the street. It has a collection of old prints and photographs inside. In the early 1900s Eastry was one of the Kent villages to set up a rat and sparrow club to keep down the numbers that had been classed as vermin. In March 1913, at this inn, members produced 630 rats' and 937 sparrows' heads. In 1919, the government began the National Rat Week and the public was urged to kill as many as possible and were paid a small fee.

ECCLES

There are four villages named Eccles throughout the country and this one was known as Aecclesse in AD 975 and is from *egles*, a Romano-British Christian church. Born at Aylesford in 1848 Thomas Buss moved to Eccles and in 1908 wrote a pamphlet about the village. At the time the local brick and cement works paid £5 a week, an enormous amount then, most of it spent on gin and beer in the pubs. A strong temperance movement grew up locally and Buss, a member, went with his father to public houses and carried away the drunks in a wheelbarrow. Although a small village in the 1930s, Eccles had its own cinema.

King and Queen, Edenbridge

RED BULL

A most unusual name for a pub and, although it takes in the Papal Bull (the lead seal on an edict from Rome: Roman Catholic inn-keepers sometimes named their pubs in deference to this), the Red Bull has some significance here. At the end of the lane on which it stands there is a Skinner's Close that may indicate a slaughterhouse, abattoir or leather-tanning place. It appears to be a sixteenth-century alehouse originally with cream and white stucco walls and enclosing beams. There are church settle-style pews and comfortable leather sofas with an agricultural implement for some curious purpose over an open fire. There is also a piano for singalongs.

EDENBRIDGE

KING AND QUEEN

Often this name was given at the time of King William and Queen Mary so this pub may have been opened between 1688 and 1694 when Mary died. The inn, opposite the old leather market, is built in white stucco with half-tiled frontage and a peg-tiled roof. Almost at the end of the High Street, there is a wealth of eighteenth-century houses, gabled and weatherboarded houses and shops. Some of the shops are of the old fashioned village shops style including a tack shop for horse people.

WHITE HORSE INN

In the town centre, this has been a coaching inn since 1574 under a Royal Charter by Queen Elizabeth I. She ordered inns to be set up throughout the county to make it easier for merchants and others to travel and trade to benefit the economy of the country. It was also the same time as the first permanent English theatre was built in London. The White Horse Inn shows its coaching inn credentials by the wide entrance at the front of the pub leading through to a courtyard. The sign has been in use since the fifteenth century and is the county emblem for Kent and a galloping white horse refers to the House of Hanover and the accession of George I in 1740. The sign is also in the arms of several guilds. The pub has connections with local rugby and bonfire societies.

YE OLD CROWN INN

Here is a fourteenth-century inn with a sign that spans the High Street; this is the only such span in Kent. Once the haunt of notorious smugglers the Ransley Gang, there is still a concealed passage they used to bring in contraband and other booty. George Ransley was born in 1782 and was, for years, a ploughman and carter. One day he found a hidden supply of spirits and other contraband which he sold and opened a pub called the Bourne Tap at Aldington. The Ransley gang was broken up in 1827 and George Ransley was transported to Tasmania where he became a successful farmer. It is white painted and brick on two storeys with a beamed gable-end and a number of bars.

EGERTON

Known as Earingtun about 1100, the farm of Ecgheard . There is the sweetest little village green here with an old village water pump and an enormous iron bowl for flowers and benches under a tree. In the part fourteenth-century church is a chandelier given to the church in 1699 and said to be the oldest such light fitting in England, possibly in the world.

GEORGE INN

High on a hill and overlooking the weald this George is right in the heart of *The Darling Buds of May* country and is a sixteenth-century building. It first opened as a pub in 1729 and traded as a 'blind pig' (that meant without a licence) until 1743. The George is one of the most popular pub names throughout the country. Originally, it referred to St George, the patron saint, and is often twinned with a dragon. However, since 1714, George has been a king's name and there have been six of them, so any pub thus named may be one of these sovereigns.

ELHAM

In 1086, this was Alham, an enclosure where eels are found. In the thirteenth century, Edward I persuaded his father Henry III to set up a market here. It was famous for hides and leatherwork before it died out in the early nineteenth century. A woman who became famous lived here for some time – the film star, Audrey Hepburn.

ABBOT'S FIRESIDE INN

Built in 1480 when Richard III was defeated and killed at Bosworth it was called the Smithies Arms when it was used by the Duke of Wellington for training while expecting a French invasion. At one time it belonged to the abbot of the monastery at nearby Lyminge and was used as a hospice.

Below the eaves, the beams are carved into grotesque human figures and there is a large lintel over the fireplace with carved dragon-like creatures. This fireplace, as well as the inn, is listed by the English Heritage Society. The inn has antique furniture (including four-poster beds), original leaded windows and massive beams. Each of the six bedrooms is named after a famous person connected with the inn such as the Duke of Wellington and Charles II. This latter gentleman is said to have stayed there when he was fleeing south after the Battle of Worcester in 1651. It is an imposing building, opening out on to the wide street that was clearly used for turning stagecoaches.

KING'S ARMS

Surrounded by Georgian, and even earlier, houses this pub is on the old market square that is just off the high street. One local always used to turn up in a pony and trap for his lunch and beer. It has one small front bar and a large dining room. The King's Arms is a sixteenth-century coaching inn with an archway to the stables. At the time of Charles II a courtier was asked which hostelry to use and was told not to go to the King's Arms as the king's arms were always full, but the king's head was empty.

Abbot's Fireside, Elham

King's Arms, Elham

ROSE AND CROWN

The fictional Scarlet Pimpernel is said to have stayed at this inn and his horse was prepared for his rides to the coast and a boat trip over to France to save aristocrats. Baroness Orczy created her fictional hero around this pub and other parts of Kent. It is a sixteenth-century coaching inn re-fronted in 1740 and was the courthouse of the Elham Petty Sessions. There is accommodation built into the old coaching stables set around a courtyard and, once, the leather market was held outside this yard. There are sofas alongside the open fire.

FARNINGHAM

Old English Ferningeham, the dwellers among the ferns. There is a hole in the side of the tomb of a Thomas Nash here and it was averred that anyone who can push a pin through it would have sight of the Devil.

LION HOTEL

This name usually comes associated with a colour such as the Red Lion and even Blue Lion that had special reference to Queen Anne. There is also a Green Lion at Rainham, Kent, but for no apparent historical reason. It stems from the heraldry of aristocrats who wished to associate their family with bravery. Overlooking the river and the eighteenth-century brick-built bridge the Lion Hotel was a staging post. There are Georgian bow windows and balconies built into the façade of the inn.

Pied Bull, Farningham

PIED BULL

A pied bull is an animal of more than one colour and there are several such pubs throughout the country. A phantom coach and horses has been heard outside this pub on the main road by people sitting at window seats. This was an old coaching road between London and Dover and the new part of the inn, which incorporates these seats, was once part of the road itself. It was opened in 1612 by Matthias Rage and he stayed there until 1638. In the seventeenth century it was described as 'A hospicium with barn and garden adjacent'. Between 1780 and 1810, they serviced six coaches a day. In 1710, the licensee was granted a 500 year lease for the water in the garden for the horses.

FAIRSEAT

VIGO

On the North Downs Way, this was originally a drovers' inn. They have a game of Dadlums, an old table skittle game unusual enough to be listed in the Guinness Book of Records. This game is played on a low platform, six feet long with miniature pins and three-inch 'cheeses' are thrown at them. It has been run by the same family since 1930. The building dates back to 1471, during the War of the Roses, and was once called the Upper Drover Inn. It takes its present name from a sea battle at Vigo Bay when the English fleet trounced the Spanish. In that battle a Fairseat man saved the life of Admiral Sir George Rooke, Fleet Commander, who bought this inn for him and the name was changed to Vigo. It was a coaching inn between Tonbridge and Gravesend. During renovations, over half a century ago, a small cupboard was found and said to have been used to hide boys when the press gangs called and contraband was hidden. Once, a scented musk that has long disappeared from England grew outside this pub.

FAVERSHAM

In AD 811 this was Fefresham, the home of the smith.

ALBION TAVERN

The length of Front Brents is a creek-side row of Victorian houses with weeping willow all along the front. At the end is the Albion with picnic tables outside. Built in 1748 it is weatherboarded and brick with tiles and much of the light comes in through large picture windows. Outside is an old ship's anchor. It has one large three sided bar overlooking the creek. Many south England pubs are called the Albion based on *albus*, the Latin for the whiteness of the coastline. There was also a territory called Albion by Sir Francis Drake in 1579 that subsequently became California and Oregon.

BEAR INN, MARKET PLACE

The bear figures in many heraldic signs, but also refers to bear baiting that was banned by the Oldham Act of 1836. Sometimes landlords chose the word because of its closeness to 'beer'. Market Place, including the Bear and ancient Guildhall, was not as safe an area once as it is now. Michael Greenwood, a schoolboy in 1748, was taken by a naval press gang there and served 12 years before the mast. He witnessed the execution of Admiral Byng in 1757 after Byng was found guilty of negligence at sea. Voltaire, the French philosopher, commented, 'In this country [England] it pays well, from time to time, to kill an admiral to encourage the others.' (Considering the fate of Greenwood a notice in the pub makes curious reading: 'Unattended children will be sold as slaves'). The Bear was owned by Thomas Arden in 1540 as an alehouse known as Le Beare and, opposite the old Guildhall, it opened with a full licence in the early 1700s and then re-built a short distance away in the 1800s. In the back bar are a carved wooden bear and a clock where the figures are replaced by the letters in the pub name. There is a public bar opening out onto the street and down a narrow low corridor are two wood-panelled snugs and a restaurant. In mid 2005, this was being considered for the CAMRA National Inventory of pubs of outstanding historic interest.

CROWN AND ANCHOR, THE MALL

Opened in the early 1800s it is one large bar with hops hanging around the room. The pub name comes from retired naval chief petty officers and derives from their arm badge of a crown and anchor. The tune for the American national anthem, *Star Spangled Banner*, originated at the Crown and Anchor, the Strand, London in 1790. That pub was used by the Ancreotic Society for singing and orchestral pieces. The music to *Ancreon in Heaven* was penned by John Stafford Smith. The Crown and Anchor, Faversham, has one large central bar with an area for darts and billiards.

HOLE IN THE WALL, PRESTON STREET

The building next door was the home of Edward Jacob, (1710-1788) the Faversham historian and one time mayor. Jacob was an early botanist and author of *Plantae Favershamienses*; a catalogue of the more perfect plants growing spontaneously about Faversham, and recorded 144 new plant records for Kent. Several explanations have been given for the pub name; that it was a hole for condemned prisoners to talk through; debtors' prisons where goods and food were passed through; or, in the case of lepers, priests would put their hands through to bless those within.

SUN INN, WEST STREET

The Sun opened its doors in 1396, in the last years of the Crusades and the year before Whittington became Mayor of London. Part of the inn has been recycled from old ships' timbers so there are many oak beams, and ceiling supports. It is in the historic West Street, right at the heart of the ancient town. The pub name is a comparatively modern one and usually means how fortunate that one has a place in the sun. It became popular because it was an easy visual sign to paint; a yellow circle with rays coming off it.

SWAN AND HARLEQUIN

In 1725, when the Order of the Bath was founded by George I, the Swan and Harlequin opened to local seamen and fishermen who lived nearby. There is legend that the brothers Crispin and Crispianus lived in the area, as there was an Elizabethan play about them, *A Shoemaker, A Gentleman*, set in Canterbury. It has not been performed in living memory. It may be that the apocryphal cobbler's tale started here. A customer collecting mended boots recently commented, 'What a fine day'. To which the cobbler replied, 'I prefer it when it rains; it's good for the leeks.' Customer, 'I suppose any rain is good for gardening.' 'No, not them leeks; the leaks in peoples' shoes'.

FOLKESTONE

A Saxon town known as Folcanstan in AD 697, from a stone marking a meeting place of Folca.

BLACK BULL

One of Folkestone's largest inns, the Black Bull opened in 1742 and now has a mock Tudor appearance. It was then outside the town and was mainly used by local farm labourers and travellers. There is a record from 1727 when it was willed to Thomas Baker and, in 1762, it was owned by the Earl of Radnor with Thomas Standley as landlord. In 1864, the Folkestone Fair was held in the pub grounds but there was some very bad behaviour. The landlord and owner were promised a spirits licence if the fair were to be closed; but the fair carried on and was described in the local newspaper as 'A hotbed of immorality and vice.' In 1905 the pub had a tea garden, bowling green, leaded lights and was well on the way to respectability.

BRITISH LION

In 1460, this inn opened up as a pilgrims' rest and was later known as the Priory Arms. There had been a priory nearby from the seventh century that was later suppressed by Henry VIII. Part of a medieval wall was discovered near this inn during renovation work. It is mentioned as an inn in 1782 in Powell's Survey with John Ladd as owner-occupier. During the Napoleonic Wars, there was an upsurge of patriotism and several pubs were named this after the British lion for courage and strength. Charles Dickens knew it well and used it when writing *Little Dorrit* in 1855. Until 1948, only four families had owned it over 120 years. It has a Queen Anne bowed front and is set in the Bayle, an historic part of Folkestone, and is surrounded by eighteenth-century cottages and large town houses. Festooned along the bar top is hop-bine while, in a fireplace, there is a large selection of porcelain, pottery and metal lions and a number of soft lions in a fire basket. Nearby there is a collection of coins that have been affixed to part of the old timber framing. At one end of the bar is a large library of books and at the other end, near a raised dais, a number of old beer pump clips. Outside, on the pavement, is a large, recumbent stone lion.

LIFEBOAT

As one would expect to find within sight of Folkestone Harbour, the Lifeboat is an eccentrically shaped pub on a corner. Opened in 1861 it is the last example of timber-framed buildings in that part of the town. The building dates back to 1750 when it was occupied by a mariner, Richard Kennett, and, in 1865, a retired schoolteacher is listed as landlord. In 1902, one landlady, Alice Setterfield, was fined £5 9s for selling beer outside licensed hours. It is a fine back street pub and is decorated with photographs of lifeboats and crews over the years. Nearby is the attractive sea front with a beach and a fish market. Inside the inn is an L-shaped bar with low ceilings in black and cream. There is a large collection of beer pump clips and the Yard of Ale glass. (A yard of ale was an eighteenth-century invention so that stagecoach drivers could have over two pints of beer without getting off their driving boards).

RED COW, FOORD STREET

Once Foord was a village outside Folkestone and this pub was called the Plough. Its present name is unusual and could have been named after a particular breed of the animal at that time. The building went up in 1692 and, as the publican proudly proclaims on a mural inside, at the time of Charles II. The first known landlord was Thomas Pay in 1741, when it was reported that a chalybeate spring had been found nearby and was reported in Seymour's Survey of Kent. It was then said to be 'In a degree equal to the Tunbridge Waters'. It has an L-shaped bar with a restaurant.

ROYAL GEORGE

As it is close to the seaside it is no surprise this was once called the Mermaid. Much of this part of the town was destroyed by a parachute mine in 1940. This inn is first recorded in 1717 when Henry Jeffrey was the licensee and it was named the Royal George in 1734 in honour of George II. It was impressive hotel, at one time, and Charles Dickens complained he was held up on a train branch line because of activities at the Royal George. One Hobson Le Butt was landlord in 1873 when he assaulted an employee, Adam Forrester. He stripped him naked and threw him out into the street because he had been late for work. He was fined. One landlady was also fined for allowing prostitution on the premises in 1890. The inn was totally rebuilt in 1984.

THISTLE AND SHAMROCK

Opened in 1525 the Shamrock and Thistle claims to be Folkestone's oldest pub and there is some history it was there in 1426. This is from documents showing that residents were paying their taxes here. There is also evidence that the Mayor of Folkestone dined here with colleagues in 1525 at a cost of 3s 4d (about 20 pence). It has had other names in the past including the George and the Cheker which, one can only suppose, was Chequer. The Thistle may well have been an old coaching inn as it is reported in 1729 that two mares had been stolen or strayed from the stables of the inn. One of two clubs that meet here is the George Inn Cork Club, who refuse to drink alcohol. The pub describes itself as a home for Celts with 'hospicalis' painted at the end of a wall painted in mauve and green, and is found up a cobbled alley. The external painting took place in 1997 and it has since been known as the Purple Palace. In the windows are a wide range of books from canary keeping to snooker and a grinning skull perched next to an old sewing machine. On the wall, near the entrance, it reads 'Come in for the Craic.'

Thistle and Sham, Folkstone

FOOTSCRAY

Named after the River Cray, a Celtic river name meaning fresh, clean water. Foots Cray was held by a man called Fot in 1086 and was known then as Fotescraet.

SEVEN STARS

A sixteenth-century timber-framed inn, it was named the Plow when the landlord was Richard Peake between 1718 and 1723. His widow changed the name to the Seven Stars between 1736 and 1751 and the present inn sign has seven stars around the Virgin Mary's head. The star was a religious symbol for either the star of Bethlehem or the Virgin Mary, one of whose titles is Star of the Sea. Some years ago, a stone carving of the Virgin's head was found down a well near the pub and is now over the fireplace in the bar. It is thought this was a church corbel or carved decoration brought down during the English Civil War.

GILLINGHAM

The Saxon homestead of Gylla. Here there is a memorial clock to William Adams, the first Englishman to have lived in Japan and who founded the Japanese Navy.

BURNT OAK

Several centuries ago there was an oak tree outside this pub that was struck by lightning, leaving a large hole in it. In the 1600s, an old witch lived in this shattered oak tree and sold charms and potions to local people. For a special fee, she weaved a magic spell around sailors so they would be faithful to their wives and sweethearts when travelling abroad. It is a large early Victorian pub on a corner surrounded by early and mid-Victorian cottages and named after the occasion 400 years ago.

WILL ADAMS

The gentleman after whom this pub was named, Will Adams, was born at Gillingham in 1564, coming from humble stock. From the age of 12, he was trained as a pilot and shipwright under Nicholas Diggins. During a Dutch expedition he finished up at Bungo, Japan and became friends with the Emperor Ieyasu. He built replica ships for the emperor and became a *hatamoto*, banner carrier in a Shogun's court. Adams spent the rest of his life in Japan although conferring with English physicians. It is a white, corner pub with oddly styled writing on the sign board. Once there was a large mural but this has been painted over.

GOUDHURST

The wooded hill of a Saxon, Gutha. In 1747 an ex-army corporal, William Stur, formed a militia and took on the Hawkhurst Gang of 100 outlaws and smugglers. This militia had found the tunnel between the inn and the church that was used by the smugglers to bring in their booty and set up an ambush. When the gang heard of the militia and their intention, they threatened to burn down every house in Goudhurst and kill everyone there. In a pitched battle, the militia beat the gang and several were arrested to be hanged later. Some of the badly wounded smugglers died in this tunnel and there have been reports of low moans and cries coming from behind the bricked up entrance. One of the leaders of the smugglers, George Kingsmill, was killed and his body buried under a skull and crossbones on his gravestone in the churchyard. In the nineteenth century James Fegan set up an orphanage for boys who were trained on local farms and then sent out to Canada.

STAR AND EAGLE

This fine brick and beamed inn, over 600 years old, comes under two religious protections. The star refers to the Virgin Mary, one of whose titles is Star of the Sea, and has been an inn sign since the fifteenth century and, since 1634, a sixteen-pointed star has appeared on the arms of the Worshipful Company of Innkeepers. The eagle part is another Christian and heraldic sign, again from the fifteenth century. The eagle has always been used as church lecterns as it was the symbol of St John the Evangelist and signifies courage. In the past the inn has been known as the Black Spread Eagle (that could refer to the Gin Act of 1786 when landlords draped their signs with black velvet and added 'black' to the pub name) and, for some time, the Olde Starre and Crowne. There used to be a winding staircase to the massive stone cellars where smugglers hid their booty and there are several bars with beams and an inglenook fireplace. There is a seventeenth-century water clock that has been wall mounted and a sundial, made by James Smythe of Salisbury in 1692, in one bar. Pub dogs are not happy about the ghost here but landlords and landladies have found a polite 'Good morning' has been enough to put it to flight.

GRAFTY GREEN

A strange name but it is probably from a grove of trees on a green. It was nearby that the famous Wooton family lived at Boughton Malherbe and one of them, an ambassador for Elizabeth I, said 'An ambassador is an honest man sent to lie abroad for the good of his country.' Later their house was inherited by the Earl of Chesterfield, who brought about the Gregorian calendar in 1742, and was accused by the peasants of robbing them of eleven days of their lives.

KING'S HEAD

A classic tale of haunting occurs in this large roadside pub in a small village. Many years ago a coach overturned and the driver and passengers were all killed. The party was on its way to this inn, where they were taken after the accident, and have taken up their ghostly residence here. Tales abound of a coach appearing on misty nights driven by a headless coachman. The King's Head was used as a safe house by Dover Bill, the smuggler. He was almost caught here when surrounded by Revenue men during a drinking session. He escaped during the gunfight that followed but several of his men were caught and hanged on Penenden Heath, Maidstone. Dover Bill was among the thousands who watched the hangings and was ostracised by all who knew him, barred from this inn from that day onwards and died in poverty. He regularly returns outside the pub and appears to be consumed with hatred. There are large murals on the external pub wall of Dover Bill and a coach running by moonlight.

GRAVESEND

In 1086, this was Gravesham, place at the end of a grove of trees or copse. It was also said to be the place where Princess Pocahontas died. She was the daughter of a chieftain and was the first American Indian to be baptised, as Rebecca. She later married John Rolfe, magistrate of the colony in 1614. They came to England with their son, Thomas, in 1616 with an escort of 12 American Indians and were received at court. She may have died of the plague and was buried at St George's church, Gravesend, aged only 21. There are stained-glass windows in the present church depicting Pocahontas and a statue in the churchyard.

THREE DAWS

A riverside inn that has been a second home for the River Thames pilots for centuries. In the olden days, it was regularly raided by the naval press gangs looking for recruits for the navy. In 1798, under Lord Nelson, the Admiralty decreed that the Three Daws was never to be raided by a single press gang; there had to be several because so many seamen escaped through its tortuous passages. There were some thirty rooms with six separate staircases. Cellars underneath the pub were used by smugglers and there were large chimneys so men could hide up them. The bird is now usually referred to as a Jackdaw but was once called simply a daw, which is the name used by Shakespeare. The acquisitive attitude of these birds has been well documented and often refers to people with an eye for the gaudy.

Pocahontas, Gravesend

Three Daws, Gravesend

GROOMBRIDGE

The village name means bridge of the horse grooms and is recorded in 1318 as Gromenbregge. There used to be a weekly market and fair at Groombridge that was instituted in 1286 under a royal charter. The fair died out in the 1900s, but the market was still held until the middle of the last century.

CROWN INN

As a pub name, this is the second most popular name after the Red Lion. Built in about 1585 it has ancient beams throughout the house and, indeed, a flying freehold. This flying freehold is a very strange area of property law. It occurs when one property, in this case the Crown, has the right to the roof space over the other houses nearby. Alongside an eighteenth-century row of cottages, all brick and tile hung, the Crown is on a sloping green with pollarded lime trees in front and timber tables and chairs for eating *al fresco*. There are inglenook fireplaces and ancient mugs and bottles hanging from the ceiling with a brass-topped bar and a view across the green from window seats to the church. One visitor might well have been author, Conan Doyle, who stayed with friends at nearby Groombridge Place. The pub is mentioned in his book, *The Valley of Death*.

Crown Inn, Groombridge

HADLOW

A Saxon mound or a hill where heather grows.

ROSE REVIVED

The inn was once just the Rose and Crown from 1509 when Henry VIII married Catherine of Aragon. It is an oak-beamed single bar with a collection of old keys and a large log fire. In the bar is a detailed history of the building. There are two stories behind this curious name of Rose Revived. One is that it was called the Rose by one landlord and then named the Crown, before going to the Rose Revived. Another story is from an Oxfordshire pub where Cromwell found a rose had died on his tunic; he put it in a pot of ale and it revived and the pub had a new name.

HALLING

In the eighth century, this was Hallingas, the farm of Heall. William Caxton is said to have married a Halling girl and set up a printing works here. In 1912, the remains of a 4,000 years old skeleton were found along with the remains of a canoe. The first county history of Kent was published by William Lambarde, *A Peramubulation of Kent*, in 1592

HOMEWARD BOUND

First licensed in 1772, it has open fires and hop vines hanging from low ceilings. 'Homeward bound' was a favoured tattoo of royal and merchant sailors, usually on the upper arm showing a four-masted ship in full sail on balmy seas. Now this is a mid-Victorian terraced pub in the village centre that was once a masons' bar. On the top floor is a round window, rather like a ship's porthole. The Medway Triumph Motor Cycle Club members meet here. The darts game at the Homeward Bound is on a traditional Kent board with no trebles.

HALSTEAD

This was a Saxon place of refuge or safety.

ROSE AND CROWN

A grade II listed building, the Rose and Crown is over 200 years old and is flint faced with two bars. It was previously called the Crown and there are pictures of the pub and village of many years ago. There is a collection of hot water bottles behind the bar and a ghost, known as Humphrey, who makes frequent appearances. The pub has a Bat and Trap team. Halstead is made up of early Victorian houses of brick and weatherboard, at least two with old iron water pumps outside and covered wells. Occasionally the Loose Women's Border Morris group dance here. This is described as a loose, loud, stompy style of dancing. The name originated in the Kent village of Loose, near Maidstone, and has been going over 25 years.

HARRIETSHAM

Either the river meadow of a Saxon called Heregard or near army quarters. A seventeenth-century gourmand lived in Harrietsham. Nicholas Wood had a vast appetite and at one sitting ate 84 rabbits and, on another greedy occasion, a whole roast pig and three pecks of damsons (about six gallons of the fruit). On one wall of a house in the village, dated 1902, there is a baker's sign and opposite, at the garage, two old Shell petrol pumps.

PEPPER BOX INN

Once the haunt of smugglers and outlaws this inn was named after their favourite weapon, the Pepper Box pistol. This pistol, invented by J.R. Cooper in 1840, fired six shots. The pub dates back to the fifteenth century and is decorated with pewter mugs and hop vines. It still has the old Sun Insurance plaque and there is an inglenook fireplace. From the terraced beer garden, shaded by trees, there are breathtaking views over Kent.

ROEBUCK

Named after the male of the roe deer, a small species of the spotted deer, that ran aplenty centuries ago. It is a white, weatherboarded brick building that was a coaching inn over two centuries ago, and part of it is listed. Inside it is enormous, completely belying its outward appearance. There is a brass foot rail that runs the length of the bar and a small collection of old, decorative teapots. For many years, there have been stories of an aged man sitting at a table in the old part of the inn who then slowly disappears. Opposite is a row of early eighteenth-century cottages where the small stream runs; one of them named Pooh Cottage.

Pepper–Box, Harrietsham   Roebuck, Harrietsham

HAWKHURST

A wooded area with resident hawks. In 1842 in the church records it was noted that 'Urinaries' should be closed at the sides of the church and a 'Necessary' opened in the parish stables next door. The famous astronomer, Sir John Herschel, lived here and a window at the church shows the wise men following the star and close to the pew he used. A former village pharmacist, Walter Pridgeon, had many home made cures such as 'All Kinds of Cough Lozenges' and 'Odontalgic Essence' to cure toothache.

EIGHT BELLS

A Kent-built classic house from the 1400s; the inn has stood here since Elizabethan days and is named after the peal of the nearby church of St Lawrence. It is at the south-eastern corner of the green and has two bars and a restaurant. Eight bells is the usual number of bells in a peal and that means the pub is a rural one and near a church. In a seaside port or town eight bells would mean the end of a watch.

OAK AND IVY

As late as 1914 this pub advertised 'Sheep taken in and good beds'. A number of the local smugglers and outlaws were captured here on one occasion and hanged at Chichester. It is an unusual name and an ivy bush used to be the favourite haunt for an owl to nest and smugglers were known as owlers in the eighteenth century. Oak apples or leaves were also used as a secret badge of passage carried by Jacobites.

ROYAL OAK

The oak tree in a pub name is usually connected with the flight of King Charles after the Battle of Worcester, when he hid in such a tree with Colonel William Carless. This Royal Oak is an ancient inn and a listed building that had to be almost rebuilt after a fire ripped through it. It is said to be haunted by a small man, seen wandering through the staff accommodation and disappearing through a wall. He has been given the sobriquet George and is thought to be same gentleman who appears as just a pair of staring eyes in one of the bedrooms.

HERNE

About 1100 this was Hyran a corner of land. In 1905, the Revd Giles Daubeney reported in his *Reminiscences of a Country Parson* that there were three old men living here who had been smugglers all their lives. The village was the inspiration for Ferne in Somerset Maugham's *Of Human Bondage*. The Revd Nicholas Ridley, as vicar here, allowed *Te Deum* to be sung for the first time in English in England. He supported Archbishop Cranmer in what were called 'corrupt and naughty opinions' and was martyred in 1555.

SMUGGLER'S INN

Over two centuries old, the top floor of the Smuggler's was once used by smugglers on the lookout for revenue men. Once there was a secret tunnel between the pub and church to bring in their booty. There are two bars with wooden beams, brassware, dried hops decorate the pub and, in one bar, is the prow of a whaler. The Kent game of Bat and Trap is played in the garden. Over a century ago four cases of rum were found at the inn and, presumed to be part of some smuggler's booty, were taken away by customs officers.

HERNE BAY

DIVER'S ARMS

In the early 1830s, a smuggler who operated from this pub was William Hooper Wood. He was caught and went to prison for five years. Then he became a licensed diver and, with the profits, took over this inn. At first, it was called Wood's Beerhouse and Wood changed it to the Diver's Arms in 1858. The inn sign carries the divers' motto, 'Where there is breath there is hope'. On two occasions, Wood was discovered to have made a way from his cellar into an adjoining brick culvert that carried the brook and the village drainage system, and then to the promenade, to bring in his smuggled brandy. Set below the inn sign is a board pointing to the North Pole, 2,675 miles away. Inside is a long narrow bar with life buoys and nautical pictures on the walls and two large pictures of the world painted on the ceiling. Behind some brass portholes are some naughty pictures.

HERNHILL

This was Har hylle, the grey hill, and Haranhyll by 1100. Underneath some nineteenth-century cottages in the village there is said to be buried treasure, hidden away by a previous church.

Diver's Arms, Herne Bay

RED LION

Built in 1364 the Red Lion is a Wealden hall house with tiles held down by iron ties and a tiled roof supported by curved bracket with two projected wings. Outside there is a wall sundial, and it is surrounded by nineteenth-century cottages and oast houses. Inside, the narrow bar is flag-stoned and there is much heavy beaming with exposed brick walls. In the early 1900s, the then landlord, Obadiah Fowler, said it had been in the family for 400 years and they had a well in the garden still in use. The inn was used for inquests after the Courtney Riots. This was the last armed uprising on British soil and took place in 1838. The poor farm labourers were starving and along came 'Sir William Courtenay' who raised an army from this lot. He was a Cornishman, John Thom, calling himself Sir William after spending some years in a lunatic asylum. There was a pitched battle at Bossenden Woods and Thom, seven of his men and two soldiers were killed. Two labourers were transported to the colonies. To mollify the locals a school was opened here and one of the little pupils was Jack Cornwall, hero of Jutland, who stood by his gun on HMS *Chester* and won a VC.

HEVER

In AD 814, this was Heanyfre, a hill brow.

KING HENRY VIII

An impressive roadside inn with half tile and brick and some oak beaming over a fine porch entrance that was once two houses. Henry VIII was a frequent visitor to this area when he was wooing Anne Boleyn. There are motifs throughout referring to King Henry and Anne Boleyn and, framed on the walls, are copies of letters between them. Typical of that period the inn has oak beams, open fireplaces and wood panelling throughout. It has stood here as an inn since 1597, soon after the invention of the water closet by Sir John Harington. Behind the inn is a secluded pond overhung by trees.

HIGHAM

In 1512 the vicar of Higham, the Revd Edward Steroper, was admonished by his bishop for having carnal relations with a nun at the Benedictine nunnery, one Lady Anchoretta Ungelthorpe. Things got so bad, with other gentlemen visiting, that the Prioress had a wall built around it. One nun there later admitted helping herself to the Common Chest to pay off family debts and two others had babies by the reverend gentleman. The legend of Dick Turpin started here at Higham. A man was robbed early one summer morning and identified his assailant, who was tried, but acquitted, because he said he was in York at 8.30 p.m. that day. Later that man described how he had ridden to Gravesend, across the ferry and on through Essex and Cambridge to York where he actually spoke to the Mayor of York to set up his alibi. Except this was not Dick Turpin and his famous Black Bess, but an infamous Kent highwayman, Swift Nick.

King Henry VIII, Hever

Stone Horse, Higham

STONE HORSE

The original building went up in the reign of George III in 1774 and, structurally, is much the same as it was then. It was owned then by Stephen Duke, a corn dealer and merchant, as a house. At one time corn mills were run by water but, occasionally, horses were attached to the top wheel to walk round in circles and this might have been 'the stone horse' and Duke named his house after that. Another story is that in the seventeenth century there was a local horse called Stone, who was famous for his strength and as a stud. A farm was named after him, Stone's House, and this farm still remains. It is an unspoiled, classic Kent country pub surrounded by trees. In 1831 Charles Hasted, a brewer and maltster, obtained a beer licence under the terms of the 1830 Beer Act that enabled any householder of good character to obtain a licence to sell beer from any dwelling on payment of two guineas to the department of excise. There is a wood panelled public bar with a log fire and much in the way of copper and brass kettles, ladles, trumpets, jugs and old blowlamps. Occasionally the Kent dance group, Copperfield Clogs, perform here.

HIGH HALDEN

Known as Hadinwoldungdenne in 1100, it was the woodland pasture of Heathuwald. The village was the seat of the Hales family and Sir Robert Hales was Lord Treasurer to Richard II at the time of the Peasants' Revolt in 1381 and later murdered by them.

CHEQUERS

Once a thatched building it has original oak beams and wrought iron ties. It is a typical Kent house with the fire in the main hall and the hall open to the roof. This was straight through to the chimney, which is why the old rafters are smoke stained. During the Peninsular War, a deserter turned up at this inn. Thomas Kirkham had walked from Spain through the Pyrenees and France and spent the rest of his life in the Chequers regaling all with his tales of war, especially a local historian.

HIGH HALSTOW

RED DOG

The Red Dog is a most unusual name for a pub and it is clearly an eighteenth-century building with a cat-slide roof. It has very low beams with a wooden floor and flagstones and a large inglenook fireplace. On the inn sign is a painted a dog, a red setter. In the village is the Old Forge where Dickens's Joe Gargery is said to have lived. At the churchyard of St Margaret's are several lozenge shaped gravestones similar to those at St James the Greater, Cooling, said to have inspired Charles Dickens to *David Copperfield*. It was said to be around here that Pip, in Great Expectations, was frightened almost to death when he came across Magwitch, the escaped convict, in a churchyard.

HOLLINGBOURNE

Holingeburna in the tenth century was from a stream of the people of Hola. Just off the North Downs and the Pilgrim's Way there is a list of vicars of the church going back to 1282.

DIRTY HABIT

Before changing its name this was the Pilgrims' Rest for pilgrims on their way to Canterbury from Winchester Cathedral. There was a building on the site between 1066 and 1085 according to the Domesday Book, demolished by an earthquake in 1382. While Chaucer was writing the *Canterbury Tales* the building was occupied by monks who put up travellers and pilgrims, one of the first inns. In 1666, it was bought by Samuel Aellard who razed it to the ground and replaced the wattle and daub with clay tiles and bricks. In the eighteenth century, a Georgian front was built on and named the King's Head. In 1975, this became the Pilgrims' Rest and, in 1992, given its present name in honour of Chaucer's humour. (Of course, the habits worn by most pilgrims would be pretty dirty by the time they got there, anyway).

HUCKING

A settlement of a man called Hucca and known as Hugginges in 1195.

HOOK AND HATCHET

A two-storey black and white inn, the Hook and Hatchet lies just off the Pilgrims' Way. It is an isolated pub down a narrow country lane and some steep hills. The name refers to the badge of a chief petty officer in the Royal Navy as, at one time, these non-commissioned officers had tree-felling rights so they could provide timber for the ships at Chatham and other dockyards. It may well have been named by a licensee retired from the Royal Navy. A hook is the nickname for an anchor and a hatchet is a small axe for chopping wood.

HYTHE

A notice from 1794 on the High Street is an injunction in stone to keep the place clean and 'prevent Boys from dirting it'. In Hythe church, there is a stack of thousands of human bones; whether they are a relic of the invasion of the Danes or the French is not known: perhaps they are from a particularly bad plague during the Middle Ages. A building, now called Centuries, was built in 1107 and extended in 1334 and 1811 that was the birthplace of Haymo, Bishop of Rochester. He founded a hospital, St Andrew's, for the poor people of Hythe in this building in 1336. In 1685, it became known as St Bartholomew's Hospital.

BELL INN
The oldest pub in town and was the main inn when Hythe was a prosperous port. Underneath the floors are tunnels to a millstream used for hiding smuggled goods. In the attic is a hook for a joist to bring in the goods fast. Parts of the inn go back to the fifteenth century and they are said to have a Grey Lady who haunts the cellars but with no story behind it. It is a corner inn with low ceilings, several bars and the most enormous inglenook fireplace for wood logs. When this fireplace was opened up for renovation some years ago the builders found old mugs, clap pipes and a bunch of keys. They also found the bodies of two revenue men who had been murdered and bricked up. It was reported at the time that their uniforms, boots and belts were still in good condition. The deeds to the premises go back over 400 years.

DUKE'S HEAD
Close to the canal, this pub is haunted by a little old man called George. His history is uncertain but even when he appears he is so diffident of manner that no one is bothered by him. In the long single bar are huge collections of cigar box tops, old soda siphons and bottles and an open fire. One couple, Bob and Dot Gifford, were licensees here for over 30 years.

KING'S HEAD
An old coaching inn it is a large single bar with a number of eating areas. An old-fashioned cooking range, well blackleaded, is a feature in the restaurant. It is a low-beamed inn with iron posts supporting the ceiling from when it was, clearly, several bars. There are a number of open fires. It has been an inn since 1513 and was known as the George in 1584, the Sun by 1714 and then the King's Head. On occasions, doors open although they have been locked and bolted. An expert in the supernatural was called in at one time and said it was the ghost of a woman called Catherine Scothers who had been a serving maid at the inn. She had died in 1897 and been buried at St Leonard's. There was also a secret meeting room here with a peephole with a small sliding door to see who was about.

WHITE HART, HIGH STREET
A huge town centre inn that was once a coaching hostelry with stabling at the rear. They have deeds, or feoffments, going back to 1648 and it is next door to the town hall. In 1648, the landlord was Fernadino Bafsooke and, behind the fireplace dogs, are the royal coat of arms.

This may well indicate that it was used by royalty on occasion. The White Hart is a flat-faced Georgian building with one of the most unimaginative inn signs I have come across: just a script with 'hart' bisecting 'white'. It was an infamous smugglers' inn and several battles took place around the inn and the narrow lanes behind it.

IGHTHAM

In 1100, this was Ehteham, the homestead of Ehta. Ightham Mote is a fourteenth-century manor house set in a deep wooded valley. There are tales that the Gunpowder Plot was hatched in a town house nearby. An American, Charles Henry Robinson, bought it in 1953 and later bequeathed it to the National Trust. An inmate at the local workhouse was Mrs Hubbard, who was said to have inspired the nursery rhyme. Over a century ago, a skeleton of a woman was found at a nearby Manor House and thought to be that of Lady Dorothy Selby. She had been walled up because of a letter she sent to her cousin, Lord Monteagle, a Roman Catholic, warning him not to attend the Houses of Parliament on 5 November 1605. It was through this the Gunpowder Plot was exposed.

GEORGE AND DRAGON

An impressive black and cream inn that was once a fourteenth-century travellers' inn sits proudly at the village centre. There was an alehouse here, originally, about 1510 and the George and Dragon, as it is now, was built in 1681. This was then enlarged in the reign of George III in 1795 when a new façade was built and an upper storey added. It is truly a beautiful old English inn with fine oak beams and inglenooks. Queen Elizabeth I is said to have visited the inn and the Duke of Northumberland was imprisoned in the old restaurant. Another guest who stayed here was Lord Stafford on his way to his public execution at Tyburn. Rather prosaically, it was called the Commercial Hotel in 1925, for a short time. Outside is a jossing block, a mounting block with three steps.

IGHTHAM COMMON

OLD HOUSE

The pub sign disappeared years ago from outside this pub and it appears as a terrace of red brick and tiled houses in a wooded dell. The advice is: open the only external door and you are in. With large open fires and exposed beams, it is sixteenth-century while other parts are seventeenth- and nineteenth-century. There is an old pre-decimal cash register in the parlour that did valiant service for over 30 years. The Old House appears in CAMRA's book on true heritage pubs. It is a Kentish red brick and tile house with piles of timber outside ready for the winter fires. There are very few pubs like this left so it would be well worth a visit before this one, along with others, disappears into history.

IVYCHURCH

Ivebrugge in the eleventh century; what else but an ivy covered church? Three hundred years ago a rector turned up at the village church but was stopped by the sexton. He told the reverend gentleman that there could be no service on that Sabbath because there was tobacco in the

Left: George and Dragon, Igtham

Below: Old House, Ightham Common

pulpit and brandy in the vestry. Many churches were used for the smuggling in those days. Along the south wall of the parish church are stone seats for the elderly and infirm before church pews came into use. Hence; 'Let the weakest go to the wall.' Pew renting was provided to raise money for the church, some for the established local gentry, a few for free and others marked For Strangers Only. The author George Orwell was most scathing of pew renters and described them as the middle class at prayer.

BELL INN

It has been a church-owned pub on glebe land for centuries and is in the shadow of the Cathedral in Romney Marshes. It is not so many years ago that strangers, turning up in this village, were treated with open rudeness in the hopes they would go away. Now it is well used by cyclists and walkers and the Bell Inn is run by a very pleasant landlord. The bell speaks all languages and, as an inn sign, it was much appreciated by sign writers over many centuries. There are so many Bell pubs it added weight to Handel's assertion that Britain was a 'Ringing Island'. From the Middle Ages a church bell would be rung when someone was dying as it kept the powers of evil away from them. It was firmly believed that there were those who would lay in wait to catch their soul at the moment of death.

KEMSING

Of Saxon origin, it was Cimescing in AD 822. Some Roman artifacts have been found, and evidence of Saxons and Jutes. A shrine was built at Kemsing to Edith, daughter of King Edgar and Wulfrith. She was known as a miracle worker and died aged 24, and her shrine attracted many religious pilgrims. There is a St Edith's well in the village still.

RISING SUN

This was a common heraldic device referring to Edward III, Richard III and many leading families. Described as an isolated hilltop pub near the North Downs, it is a converted hunting lodge. The large bar has an open fireplace guarded by an African parrot. Agricultural implements are on display and it has spectacular views over the North Downs. The sun, although a comparatively modern inn sign, is a popular one because it has a huge visual impact and indicates that the good days have arrived.

KINGSGATE

CAPTAIN DIGBY

Out on a cliff overlooking the sea with a long history it was once Bede House or the Chapel of St Peter, and later became a wayfarers' hospice and then an inn. It is now the oldest licensed pub on Thanet. Digby was a midshipman who served on the *Badger* under Captain McUllock, the first to suppress smuggling in the area when the new coast blockade started in 1816. The pub was once called the Noble Captain Digby. In 1769, the Battle of Botany Bay took place nearby when revenue men ambushed Joss Snelling and his gang as they unloaded their booty. Snelling and four others escaped through an opening in the cliffs. A riding officer was shot on the cliffs and taken back to this pub where he died and still haunts the place. Snelling, born in 1741, was fined £100 for smuggling at the age of 89. He died aged 96 and had been introduced to the future Queen Victoria as the 'famous Broadstairs smuggler.'

Black Robin, Kingston

KINGSTON

The most valuable Anglo-Saxon treasure ever found in this country was uncovered by the Rev. Bryan Faussett, curate here between 1767 and 1773 when he excavated 300 early Saxon graves alongside the old Canterbury Road. It was found in a grave dated to AD 639 and made of gold set with garnets, blue glass and shell and is now in the Liverpool City Museum. The brooch appears on the village sign. Boules is played on the bed of the dried up river, which only floods when some disaster is about to occur.

BLACK ROBIN

The inn was named after a highwayman who terrorised this area until he was caught and hanged. A life size effigy of Black Robin stands in the lounge bar of the inn. The pub is a grey painted building on two storeys containing two main bars with bare brick walls, wood panelling and large brick fireplaces. It is said to be haunted by the daughter of a former landlord who was murdered nearby.

KNOCKHOLT

In 1197, this was Ocholt, the oak tree place and Nocholt by 1153. They still have a man trading as an oak-wright in the village. Beware: as a cyclist or walker, the village is a good two miles away from the railway station.

HARROW INN

A country inn on one of Kent's highest points; it is built of brick with weatherboarding and dates back to the late 1500s. There are some superb small arched windows, similar to the Dering windows of Pluckley. It is next door to a beamed barn that is now the restaurant. In 1867, it was known as the Arrow, with a memorable ditty on the inn sign. In the early 1700s, a highwayman arrived, robbed everyone present and helped himself to all the takings. He was tracked to another inn where he was drinking the proceeds of his crime, taken back and hanged from a beam at the Harrow. From time to time, he is seen wandering about in tricorne and long black cloak. Outside is an 'iron' with a signpost on it. An 'iron' was the Victorian name for any green patch in a village shaped as a triangle because they maintained it looked like a flat iron, then used domestically and at laundries.

TALLY HO

On its own, and separated from the village, the Tally Ho is a former coaching house built on a former alehouse. The name is after the Norman French cry used in the hunt meaning 'There he goes' as they pursued Brer Fox. The Tally Ho has a whitewashed exterior with a large garden and tree shaded seats and tables. Inside it has dark wood panelling and a beamed ceiling trailing hop vines. There is a growing collection of banknotes from all over the world extending along one beam. The bar is square shaped and has a central island for service. As this is a hunting-style pub, it is appropriate to have a pair of antlers over the fireplace with a row of differently sized hunting horns. Not too far away is Down House, where Charles Darwin lived with his family and worked on the theories that culminated in his *On the Origin of Species by Means of Natural Selection* in 1859.

LAMBERHURST

Lamburherste in the 1100s, a wooded area where lambs were washed. It is a most attractive village in a dell with Georgian and early Victorian houses and a nice selection of shops for a village of its size. Many of the houses are white brick and weatherboarded and some have Mansard roofs. In 1997, the largest apple ever grown in Britain was picked here, weighing in at over 25lb. In more Rabelasian style, a vicar of Lamberhurst, Dorman Okenlane, appeared before the Bishop of Rochester's Consistory Court in the fifteenth century. While at a private party, he took an ale pot and, under the table, urinated into it. He then passed it the host, Thomas Coggar. This gentleman threw the pot at Okenlane's head and there was a fracas. Okenlane was obliged to resign, travel as a penitent to Rochester Cathedral and glaze a window there at his own expense.

CHEQUERS

The Chequers is an ancient inn sign, possibly used by the Romans for their roadside *tabernae* throughout England during their occupation. There is some evidence it was used as a sign at Pompeii for a place where games could be played. Later it was used to indicate that money could be changed and the word 'exchequer' once meant a type of chessboard. This is a fine fourteenth-

Tally Ho, Knockholt

century roadside inn although the original manor, on which it was built, went up in 1137. In 1682 it was rebuilt to appear much as it is now with some remains of the old wattle and daub. It has red hung tiles, dormer windows and a fine pitched roof with white painted brick while inside are stone-flagged floors and hop vines hanging. There is a handsome two-pillar portico entrance to the hotel and an extremely wide door into the main bar. This may well have been needed to carry in coach passengers' luggage and boxes. Ancient beams have been renovated and there are large inglenook fireplaces. As a coaching inn, it was on the three-day London to Hastings coach run and had stabling for 58 horses. The last coach to go through was in 1913; Pickford's Removals.

SWAN ON THE VINEYARD

Slightly outside the village, the Swan backs on to a vineyard, hence, the name. It is a long cream building with very low ceilings inside, several open fires and flagstones. There is a selection of books, stone hot water jugs and kitchen bottles on the windowsills. It is clear from the outside that there used to be some stabling and there are flowers in long boxes on stilts.

Chequers, Lamberhurst

LENHAM

Leanaham in AD 858, homestead of Leana. When a fifteenth-century house was restored here in 1946 there were found three bodies and weapons judged to be centuries old. One woman buried in the churchyard is Mary Honeywood, who died in 1620 with 327 descendants; 16 children, 114 grandchildren, 188 great-grandchildren and 9 great-great-grandchildren. She had lived through six reigns. Lenham Square was granted the original market charter in 1206 by King John. The square has been used on many occasions as a film location and they even have their own Town Crier.

DOG AND BEAR

A former coaching inn, the Dog and Bear was built in 1602 as Shakespeare's Hamlet was first performed and the inn was visited by Queen Anne in 1704. Since then there has been a royal coat of arms above the door. The name might signify the end of bear baiting by the Oldham Act of 1835 but the bear also has significant heraldic meaning in noble families. One such bear

Dog and Bear, Lenham

referred to Richard Nevill, Earl of Warwick, known as the Kingmaker in Shakespeare's *Henry IV*. This inn on the square is surrounded by Georgian and timber-framed medieval houses.

RED LION

Opposite Lenham Square the Red Lion is a fourteenth-century inn surrounded by Georgian and Victorian houses. A ghost, seen here on many occasions, is dressed in the seventeenth-century style and thought to be an aged pilgrim. A second ghost here is said to be an earlier landlord. In the bar there is a 1920s-style photograph showing an elegant gentleman. It reads, 'Uncle Bert, In the past and in the present'. The word 'present' is written in shivery writing to indicate that uncle Bert is still about the place. This was a resting inn for pilgrims on their ways to and from Canterbury. An old Fremlins pub, it was on the old turnpike and coaching route. Inside there is Fat Man's Alley leading to the men's lavatory.

LOOSE

In the eleventh century, this was recorded as Hlose or pigsty.

WALNUT TREE

The two bars here form an unusual L-shaped room and there is an even more unusual collection of 67 chamber pots hanging from the ceiling along with lavatory chain pulls and flintlock rifles hang over the bar. In the second limb of the bar are water jugs. One etched glass door says Private Bar, again a most unusual feature these days. Horse brasses and some horse tackle also adorn. The pub name, Walnut Tree, has always been a popular one in Kent and a variant on this is Bannut Tree. (Next door is Cut Loose, hairdressers.)

LUDDESDOWN

Hludesduna in the tenth century, the hill of Hlud.

COCK INN

Early records show that this was the Cock in 1713 and a farmhouse and alehouse prior to that. It is a large black and white inn surrounded by woodland and well known to hikers and ramblers off the Weald Way. It displays Second World War and classic car memorabilia and there are a large number of supporting timbers and huge log fires. There is a small lounge with leather armchairs and a collection of books and in a nearby alcove, an upright Olivetti typewriter in case the muse should suddenly strike a passing writer. The ceiling is covered with beer mats from all over the country and an exhibition for classic car buffs. Outside, on the walls, are small, old, metal advertisements for Persil, Ex-Lax and Weck, a German preserving jar.

LYDD

In AD 744, this was known as Hlidum, meaning, possibly, the place at the gates.

DOLPHIN

An ancient inn with low ceilings, it was once owned by Thomas a Becket (Archbishop of Canterbury) when it was included in an estate. The dolphin was looked upon by seamen as a friendly creature that would twine itself around an anchor chain in a storm to prevent it dragging. Because of this, it was frequently used as the name of a ship and especially those of the Royal Navy from 1648 to the present. A dolphin features in many coats of arms including the Fishmongers' Company and the Company of Watermen and Lightermen. There is a resident ghost at this inn and not a straight wall in the place.

GEORGE HOTEL

Not so many human phantoms here – just cats. That is enough for any dog that comes across them and they flee in complete disarray. During a battle between smugglers and revenue men John McKenzie, a young naval officer, was killed by one of the Aldington Gang, known as the Blues. The leader, Cephas Quested, was captured and hanged and McKenzie still haunts the area. The inn is said to be about 300 years old but parts of it go back to 1420 and a previous landlord carried the unfortunate surname of Lepper.

LYNSTED

Known in 1212 as Lindestede, a place where lime trees grow.

BLACK LION

A large village pub with several bars one with inglenook and large brass cooking kettles and a wild boar's head. Inside there are advertisements for Capstan cigarettes, brass portholes and a large coaching clock. It was built early in the nineteenth century on the site of an earlier inn and behind it now stands Peninsular Terrace. On a wall plaque outside, it reads that the black lion was a particularly ferocious brand of a venereal disease and often said to have been acquired in public houses. The parish church, next door, has a shingle roof and wooden spire and yew trees in the churchyard. On the military guardhouse-shaped building at the side of the pub has been painted a soldier from the Peninsular campaign.

MAIDSTONE

Maeghan stan in the late tenth century, the stone where maidens gathered.

PILOT

A grade II listed building with three bars connected to form one large bar and a log fire. It is the second oldest in Maidstone, having been built in the late 1600s. There is a jug collection and headgear pinned to the beams. Customers are invited to buy from a shelf of books for local charities. The Pilot is on a split-level with hops hanging around the bar and a U-shaped drinking area. There is a very large inglenook fireplace with wooden logs and an ancient tree feller's saw leaning in the corner. Shuffleboard is available on request to the landlord and there is a piano for singalongs.

ROYAL ALBION

It was at this inn that General Fairfax took the surrender of the Royalist army in June 1648. The last battle was in Havock Lane. It is haunted by Haughty Ann, the beautiful daughter of a previous landlord who was courted by many, but spurned them all. She said she would remain a virgin rather than marry what was on offer. She died of a fever shortly afterwards and is said to have returned looking for a likely young man. It is also haunted by Martin Shotwood who made another landlord's daughter, Sarah Oake, pregnant and then made off leaving her distraught. She drowned herself and he hanged himself. At present, it is part of a large renovation scheme in the town.

YE OLDE THIRSTY PIG

A large corner pub on the delightfully named Knightrider Road, it has all the appearances of being a genuinely old pub rather than having had a 1920s makeover in the 'brewer-bethan' style. The public bar is mockingly called the Trough whereas the front bar is The Snug; so, clearly for a better class of person. Both entrance doors are small but wide with heavy black knockers and there are dormer windows on the second floor.

MARGATE

It was known as Meregate in 1254 and meant, possibly, a gate or gap leading to the sea. Roman coins from the reigns of Oribus and Maximanus were found in a field near the town by a farmer in 1724. After defeating the Spanish Armada, Lord Howard of Effingham pulled in to Margate to send his reports to Queen Elizabeth. The town had a reputation for strong ale and John Evelyn records it as 'a certain heady ale', while Pepys said 'I foxed him with Meregate ale'. Margate was the first of the Thanet towns to introduce sea bathing by Dr Russell in 1750 and, in 1761, Benjamin Beale invented the bathing machines and sold sea water as a health cure.

BULLS HEAD, MARKET PLACE

An imposing four-storey inn where the comedian Eric Morecambe held his wedding reception when he married the landlord's daughter. She was Joan Bartlett, who had been Miss Margate and Miss Kent. It has one large island bar serving different sections of the inn, containing nautical pictures, an Edwardian coat and umbrella stand and a parrot that greets every customer as they arrive and depart. Several old wine barrels are used as tables on bare wood floors and it is lit by old-fashioned orb lights. Right opposite is the old town hall and, on the other corner, is an old-fashioned pawnbroker with the traditional three brass balls high on a wall on the first floor.

GEORGE HOTEL, KING STREET

This fine old coaching inn is not as old as the Tudor house across the road from it although it does date from the mid-eighteenth century. There used to be a large public room at this inn used for local farm and property auctions. The leaded glass lights still advertise Cobbs Ales and Stouts. The brewery for this old Kent ale was just across the road in King Street. It is clear from the adjoining stable and coach house that the George was a main coaching inn in Margate. The hotel was bombed in June 1943 and the present entrance is built into the old bowed window space. The bedroom above the bar is said to be haunted by a middle-aged woman dressed in the style of the 1940s. She is thought to have been injured or killed in the German raid over the town but there are no reports of any victims,

NORTHERN BELLE, MANSION STREET

To find this ancient pub requires some determination and skill. It is not listed in the Margate list of pubs; it is not in the telephone directory and Mansion Street does not appear in the Kent Town Centre Maps. The best way is to find Fort Hill and look for a local person. It is Margate's oldest pub and was originally cottages for fishermen in 1680. It was named after an American ship, the *Northern Belle*, which ran aground in 1857 and foundered on Ness Rock. The *Victory* lugger set sail to help the stricken ship and was struck by a tremendous sea and turned over. All nine crew perished in sight of hundreds of the town's people. Inside the inn are a series of small rooms with a narrow bar, low beams with small pewter pots hanging and a wooden floor. Truly a hidden treasure. It is said to be haunted by a woman with a very pale face wearing a white shroud. She has been seen in the bar and cellars (once used by smugglers) and was first recorded by the landlord, Robert Edward Brockman, in 1869. In the past, it has been known as the Seafarers Tavern, the Watermans Arms, (1852) and the Auroroa Borealis after that. This last name was changed when a drunk was brought before the magistrates and said he had been treated to drinks at the 'Roreborearelish'.

George Hotel, Margate

Northern Belle, Margate

MARSHSIDE

GATE INN

The pub name refers to the old gateway to the Archbishop of Canterbury's manor house which stood nearby. It is an ancient pub set in farmland on the edge of the salt marshes (hence the name of the hamlet) with two connected bars, tiled floors and is hung with hop vines. Old photographs of village people and cricket teams from the past adorn the bar walls. In the beer garden is a duck pond, a stream and apple trees. The landlord had been here 30 years in 2005. The Kent traditional entertainment includes mummers, hooдеners and Morris dancers.

MATFIELD

Mattefeld in 1230, the open land of Matta

WHEELWRIGHT'S ARMS

An early seventeenth-century pub on the edge of the village; it has its own cricket team that plays on the nearby green. It is a typical Kent pub on two storeys with white painted brick and weatherboarding. In one bar is a huge, old cart wheel to which has been added a seat and legs to form an unusual settle. Among old photographs is one in sepia of a Victorian gentleman with whiskers and stovepipe hat entitled The Hop Counter. These inns were named after the men who made the wooden wheels for carts and other tools, and the Worshipful Company of Wheelwrights was a livery company dating from 1669.

MEOPHAM

In AD 788, this was Meapaham, the homestead of Meapa. It is the longest village in Kent and pronounced 'meppum'. The cricket ground is said to be 250 years old. The black, wooden, smock mill overlooking the green, is one of the best preserved in Kent. The Meopham windmill was built in 1801 by the Killick brothers using timber from old ships at Chatham dockyard. One of the most famous residents of the village was Simon de Meopham, who became Archbishop of Canterbury in 1327. There is tale of a headless monk who walks between the Cricketers and the church.

CRICKETERS INN

Said to be oldest formal cricketing inn still existing in the country, it took its name when the Meopham Cricket Club was formed in 1776 and this was their headquarters. Cricket is (or was) the national summer game, and, as a result, there are many pubs throughout the country named after the game in many and varied ways. As early as 1735 cricket was well established in this village and there was a pub called the Eleven Cricketers, which is the earliest reference to any pub name connected with the game. Before this, the Eleven Cricketers had been called the Swan. No longer used as a pub this building still remains as a private residence. At the Cricketers Inn, there is a small public bar with a long restaurant and bar decorated with cricketing pictures, hunt pictures and an early golfing woman. The side of the pub is haunted by a woman who hanged herself when her Napoleonic Wars soldier-husband returned with a French mistress. A local miller, Bob Bennett, who hanged himself in the nineteenth century, has been seen on the green opposite the King's Arms and near the church.

Cricketers, Meopham

GEORGE INN

The oldest of the village inns is the George Inn which dates back to 1688, about the same time that Lloyds of London was set up as Edward Lloyd's Coffee bar and John Bunyan died. The George is on the right-hand side of the road going into the village from the west and is a white stucco and weatherboarded inn on two storeys. It has a steeply pitched roof and Victorian sash windows with an interesting bowed window at the side of the building.

MEREWORTH

Meranworth in AD 843, this was the enclosure of Maera, now pronounced Merryworth. The Honourable John Fane (later Earl of Westmoreland) had Mereworth Castle designed in the Palladian style and, because it overlooked the village, had the village removed half a mile so he could not see it. In 1755, Fane entertained Prince Charles, the Young Pretender, at this castle and that was the last Jacobite council. In 1854, the Baltic War brought a Victoria Cross to a resident here. Charles Lucas, later Rear Admiral Lucas, was on the HMS *Hecla* when it was shelled. He picked up the shell, with the fuse still burning, and threw it overboard.

QUEEN'S HEAD

Elizabeth I was the subject of many inn signs but she was not always best pleased with the results. Investigators were sent out to check the signs and, if they were displeased by them, they were knocked down and burnt. By Royal Proclamation of 1563, all signs showing the Virgin Queen had to be approved. A coffin maker in the village owned this pub at one time. He was making his own coffin when he collapsed over it and expired. Every now and again, his restless spirit returns to finish off the job and loud knocking sounds can be heard. (One customer maintained that it was the winner of the 1923 hide and seek game who was making the noises.)

NEWENDEN

Newedene, a new woodland pasture. Prince Edward (later Edward II) was in this village in the mid-1300s and encouraged to play 'creag' with his friends. No one knows, for sure, what this game was, but cricket historians have maintained this was the start of cricket.

WHITE HART

Opened in the late 1500s with oak beams there is a large inglenook fireplace in the main bar and an ornately carved bench. It has (perhaps) the lowest ceiling in Kent pubs; about five feet ten inches. (This always leads to the argument that people were much smaller, even a century ago). The White Hart, as a pub name, goes back to the beginnings of the reign of Richard II in 1377 as his heraldic symbol. All of his household staff wore this device and it became a common thing for innkeepers to show their allegiance in this manner, too. It is a two bar inn with a ghost that haunts the dining rooms. There are regular boat trips organised by the pub between the White Hart and Northiam Castle and there is a boules pitch outside

NEWNHAM

GEORGE INN

Found on the back slope of the downs in a one street hamlet, the George was built in 1540 as a farmhouse. It then belonged to Thomas Hart, Gentleman of Faversham, and, by the eighteenth century was a coaching house. It was named after George I. There are three inglenook fireplaces inside and there are displays of butterflies, stuffed birds, old clay pipes and cabinets holding glass bottles. It is weatherboard and brick with a white picket fence. Across the road is a vineyard. The George was part of the church estate and a brew-house for labourers, farmers and travellers. They sold beer for church funds such as Bride Ales, Church Ales and Dead Ales to signify weddings, births and deaths. It became a licensed inn in 1718 as the pirate Edward Teach (Blackbeard) was killed off the coast of North Carolina.

NEW ROMNEY

The Romney, Hythe and Dymchurch Railway, stretching 14 miles, was opened on 16 July 1927 for the local people and tourists. Smuggling wool was a full time occupation for many men. It was known as owling, and was rife from the 1300s until 1724. This was when the French found they could get cheaper wool in Ireland. The author Richard Barham said of this area: The World is divided into five parts; namely Europe, Asia, Africa, America and Romney Marsh.

CINQUE PORTS ARMS, HIGH STREET

Built in the sixteenth century, it was named after the five ports; Hastings, Romney, Hythe, Dover and Sandwich. These were chartered by the king to provide ships and men to defend England against foreign invasion from about 1155. Because of silting, the only two working ports now are Dover and Hastings. It is a long, low pub at the western end of town on two floors with a steeply pitched, tiled roof and casement windows. There are several small bars, an open log fire, and a bell on a spring behind the door to announce customers. They have a Bat and Trap team.

NEW INN, HIGH STREET

Dating from about 1381, when the first English Navigation Act was passed, this is a large inn in the middle of the town. There is a Tudor doorway and an eighteenth-century staircase. The name indicates it was built on an earlier inn. At one time, it was a posting office for the Customs and Excise men. Local legend has it that a young girl hanged herself at the New Inn in unrequited love and her ghost can still be seen walking in rooms and along passageways. It is a large town inn next door to the old school and a few yards away from the ancient town hall.

SHIP HOTEL, HIGH STREET

The Ship Hotel was first built in 1492 as Columbus sailed for the Americas and was later used by smugglers. When it was part of the Cinque Ports the sailors, who lived nearby, were entitled by statute to 'soc and sac, tel and team, bloodwit and fledwit, pillory, tumbril, flotsum, jetsum and ligun, mundbryce waives and strays'. In fact, anything they wanted from the sea. Because of their lawlessness, this even meant wrecking, grounding, plundering other ships and smuggling. The hotel is a large three-storey building at the eastern end of the town with several bars.

OARE

In Saxon times this was known as Ora, shore or hill slope. There is a UFO sightings office locally but they are extremely difficult to contact. The Vikings used the nearby Isle of Sheppey to invade the Kent mainland and the Romans were there before them. The Norse invaders described the area as 'pirates hiding up creeks'.

SHIPWRIGHT'S ARMS

Out on the marshes on the water's edge of the River Swale this inn is three centuries old and has traces of an earlier building going back to the thirteenth century. It was first licensed in 1738 when George III was born. The inn was also a Revenue Cutter Station, which would not have best pleased the smugglers and other ne'er-do-wells, who much preferred to keep their work out of sight. It still acts as a listening post for mariners in distress and the present landlord is a volunteer coastguard. Until recently, the inn generated its own electricity but they still draw water from their own well. Next door is a boatyard and the Shipwright only stocks Kentish beers and these beers are on gantries behind the bar. (One of their beers is Shipwrecked from Goachers). This may have something to do with the story behind the ghost that haunts the inn. In the nineteenth century, the captain of a ship that sank in the creek on Christmas Eve managed to pull himself ashore and over the bank that protects the pub. He died of exposure before he was found next day. When he does make an appearance there is said to be the strong smell of rum and tobacco. The bars are filled with nautical memorabilia, including the figurehead of a pirate from the Old Rye Brewery, and there is a library of books.

Shipwright's Arms, Oare

OTFORD

Otteford in AD 832, the ford of Otta. It is just off the Pilgrim's Way with a spring-filled pond in the middle of the village and the smallest listed building in England; a duck house. The ducks are fed from an allowance from the parish council

BULL

There are two roundel portraits taken from the Tudor Archiepiscopal Palace at Otford in this inn, said to be those of Henry VIII and Queen Catherine. There is a high backed oak settle here said to have belonged to Thomas a Becket, the murdered Archbishop of Canterbury, and customers are invited to sit in it and make a wish. The Bull was granted a licence by a Papal Bull from Otford Monastery; hence the name. The Victorian face hides a Tudor framed building and there are two large stone fireplaces with much panelling. An old grandfather clock measures time

CROWN

In the sixteenth century, this was two cottages and became an alehouse about 1860. It is at one end of an attractive high street and right opposite the village pond that has the Norman church behind that. Built on two storeys with a long tiled roof it has several bars and an entrance up railed steps. There are four inter-connecting rooms with beamed ceilings, and upright and wall timbers around two huge inglenook fireplaces. The cream painted walls are decorated with old prints and photographs of the village. The Crown is the second most popular name for an inn and has been used for the past 600 years. It is a simple, visual symbol and demonstrates loyalty to the contemporary monarch. This sign and name disappeared, obviously, during Cromwell's time in power, but came back rapidly afterwards.

HORNS

Once three cottages it is a timber framed building from the sixteenth century. It is tile hung with brickwork and dormer windows. Inside are heavy beams and the Horns is opposite a medieval hall house. The name can refer to deer hunting, or the post horn of the stagecoaches. Built on two storeys with a high pitched roof and dormer window it has railed steps leading into it. Opposite is an ancient protected building in Tudor style.

PADDLESWORTH

In the eleventh century this was known as Peadleswurthe, the enclosure of a man called Paedel.

CAT AND CUSTARD POT

Once upon a time there was a Red Lion here until the old sign blew away. Then along came the village artist and painted, in gorgeous colours, a sprawling lion, or was it a cat? Anyway, it became a well-known inn nicknamed the 'Cat'. At one time, the East Kent Foxhound Hunt met up there and they called it the Cat and Mustard Pot, as an inn was so called in the sporting volumes of Yorricks. This eventually became the Cat and Custard Pot as the pub name. It is a one bar country pub with pictures of the Battle of Britain. The key to the parish church is kept on a special hook at the pub.

Black Horse,
Pembury

PEMBURY

Peppingeberia in 1100, fortified home of the Pepa family. A German motorist crashed his car here and told friends about it at the Fanum Club, London, and they decided to form the Automobile Association. The first thing they did was to set up a gas lamp on Pembury Corner. The first woman to be burned at the stake at Tonbridge, during the Marian persecutions, was Margery Polley of Pembury in 1555. Her memorial is a horse trough erected in 1909.

BLACK HORSE

Obviously an old coaching inn, the Black Horse is tile hung and, inside, furnished with old pews and a log fire and is on the main street. The black horse has been a popular pub name since the fourteenth century and, by the seventeenth century, was the sobriquet for the 7th Dragoon Guards who wore black collars and cuffs on their uniforms and rode large, black horses. The inn sign, itself, is quite outstanding. They also have a noted fish restaurant.

Daylight Inn, Petts Wood

CAMDEN ARMS

The Camden dynasty was a notable political and aristocratic family in the early eighteenth century and Charles Pratt was the first Earl of Camden and a lord chancellor. His eldest son, Jeffrey Pratt, Marquis of Camden, was a lord lieutenant of Ireland for several years and, later, secretary to the colonies. The family owned the land that was developed as Camden Town in North London and gave the family name to another village in Kent, Pratt's Bottom. The Camden Arms is a large, old, former coaching inn that had extensive stabling facilities. The inn sign carries the arms of the 4th Marquess Camden, then living at Bayham Abbey.

PENSHURST

A wooded hill of Pefen recorded in 1072. Sir Philip Sidney, the Elizabethan poet and a favourite of Elizabeth I, was born here. Penshurst Place goes back to the fourteenth century and has a unique hall with large staterooms and Tudor gardens. There is a half-timbered house in the village called Poundsburge Manor that has always been known as the Pitcher House. At some time, in years gone by, it was an off-licence and the landlord served beer and cider from a pitcher through an open window.

LEICESTER ARMS

Opposite the entrance to Penshurst Place, home of the Sidney dynasty, the inn sign shows the arms of that family. Elizabeth I was a friend of the Sidney family and often visited them at Penshurst Place. The precise arms on the inn sign are those of Viscount Lisle, who became Lord Leicester in 1618. The inn was once known as the Porcupine after the arms of that Lord Leicester, showing a porcupine and a lion on either side of a pheon. The pheon was a broad arrowhead shape invented by Henry Sidney, a Master of Ordnance, to stamp on, and identify, government property. This was most publicly shown as the arrow on the clothing of convicts. A three-storey inn, it is timber framed and has much interior beaming, a large inglenook fireplace, stained-glass windows and overlooks the river at the rear. (They also have four-poster beds available; and a live parrot in the long bar).

PETT BOTTOM

A pretty enough village but comes from Old English *pytt*, a pit.

DUCK INN

Once a shepherd's cottage on the estate it was built in 1621. It was an alehouse and grocer's shop in 1849 and, later, Ian Fleming, author of the James Bond books, was a regular customer at the Duck Inn. He featured this pub in his book, *Moonraker*. There used to be a separate 007 bar with stripped pine floorboards, oak pews and mahogany tables and chairs. This, alas, has dropped its name. In the lounge is a seventeenth-century fireplace and the bar is hung with hops. Once it was known as the Woodman's Arms and it was about the time Fleming was writing about it that it acquired its unusual name. It may have been a play on words because the doors were so small. It is half tile hung with brickwork and white painted.

PETTERIDGE

HOPBINE

An old tile hung and weatherboarded inn; it has an L-shaped bar with a central fireplace. Until 60 years ago, it was a beer only off-licence. Local actors put on displays in the garden in the summertime. The bine is a flexible shoot that grows over poles or wires, especially the hop. (A 'hop pocket' is a large sack holding half a hundredweight of fresh hops that are kept for a year after being dried before they are ready for use). Some pubs in Kent are called the Hop Pocket.

PETTS WOOD

DAYLIGHT INN

Now we have William Willet to thank for clocks going back and forth in spring and autumn. Willet (1856-1915) lived near Petts Wood and advocated the Daylight Lighting Scheme for British Summertime. It was adopted as a wartime measure in 1916 and made permanent in 1926. A huge village centre pub it was rebuilt with beams in 1935. It is a good example of what became known as 'brewer-bethan' style.

PLAXTOL

A good omen for this village as it is from the Old English *Pleg stow*, a place for play or sport and known as Plextole in 1386. Until the early 1950s when people used distemper for the interior of their homes there was a blue dye used locally called 'roughway blue' but this has disappeared under layers of wallpaper.

GOLDING HOP

The interior of this ancient village pub has whitewashed walls with old oak beams and log fires. On the outside is a terraced garden overlooking a stream. There was a factory in the village that made special paper for the Bank of England notes. The pub is named after the golding hop that goes into beer. Built in the fifteenth century by 1957 it was still lit by oil lamps and water had to be brought in from nearby Sheet Hill Spring. Shaded by trees it is most colourful with flowers. It is outside the village down a winding lane and there is a huge children's playground with a stream running past.

PLUCKLEY

Land belonging to the Saxon, Plucca. The Dering window is famous throughout Kent and came about from a nineteenth-century Sir Edward Dering. He had every window in the village altered to give rounded lights under an exterior arch. The window shape had originated before the English Civil War and an earlier Dering jumped through such a window to escape the Roundheads. These arched window frames were all painted white because, Sir Edward maintained, this was lucky. The village has been reported as being the most haunted in the country. At one point there was said to be 12 ghosts still wandering about including a phantom coach and horses, black dogs, White Ladies, a Red Lady, and a man who screams. When an earlier Lady Dering died she was buried in three coffins to keep her young and beautiful forever. However she escaped the coffins and wanders the church with a red rose in her hand. Another Lady Dering is seen wandering looking for a child she lost at birth.

BLACK HORSE

At the Black Horse, there are reports of goods going missing on a regular basis only to be replaced in the same position later. The landlord of the Walnut Tree, Aldington, says that a woman he knew was working at the Black Horse and put down her handbag and cardigan in the same place every day. One day they went missing and two years later to the day there was a knocking at the door, although no one was there, and shortly afterwards, the cardigan and bag were found where they had been left previously. The poltergeist here is a woman called Jessie Brooks who was killed in the skittle alley when the pub was in a different part of the village. When it moved she moved with it, almost 200 years ago, and she is seen wandering looking for a child she lost according to the legend. This Black Horse has a long cat-slide roof with dormer windows on the second floor and, of course, Dering windows.

BLACKSMITHS ARMS

Although this is an ancient pub, it was a tearoom for a short time and featured in the television series *The Darling Buds of May*. Originally fourteenth-century it has old beams, open fires, horse brasses and hop vines. Because it is a heavily haunted pub, it was also used in a television series *Strange but True*. One ghost is a miller who had been a customer and hanged himself in the fields

Black Horse,
Pluckley

at the back in unrequited love. Another haunting the pub is an old gypsy woman who set fire to herself when a spark from her pipe dropped on to her gin soaked shawl. Another phantom is that of a coach and horses travelling between Charing and Smarden which passes the front door.

DERING ARMS

An imposing inn that was built as a hunting lodge for the Dering family; there is still the ostler's bell for those arriving by horse. There are extremely high and vaulted ceilings throughout and the main bar is heavily beamed and with flagstones. They have their own ghost, an old woman sitting in the bar in Victorian garb. The Dering windows are especially notable at this inn. The parish church is close to the inn and, on a recent visit by the Paranormal Society, curious things happened when they saw and recorded some unusual activity. As A.E. Bates readers will know, Pluckley is the home of Pop Larkin and his post-Second World War family. It was in this series of *The Darling Buds of May* that the international star, Catherine Zeta Jones, made her name and may well have been one of the many actors and film crew who used this inn.

Derring Arms, Pluckley

QUEENBOROUGH

Edward III renamed the village of Bynne after his wife Queen Phillipa as Queneburgh and built Queenborough Castle in 1361. A constable here was John of Gaunt, whose red lion bearings gave rise to 600 pubs being named after them.

FLYING DUTCHMAN

There are several inns throughout the country named the Flying Dutchman and it is usually after the legend of the ghostly ship that is supposed to haunt the Cape of Good Hope luring other ships onto the rocks and destruction. The inn sign here shows the ship in full sail. There was a racehorse called the *Flying Dutchman* that won the Derby in 1849 and often it is this horse that appears on the sign. A large village centre inn it is near the river and foreshore.

OLD HOUSE AT HOME

This name came from a Victorian ballad that told of soldiers and sailors yearning for home from abroad. One such pub at Edenbridge, Kent, showed a pig with a pipe in his mouth leaning over the wall of his sty. The Queenborough Old House is the home of the local Monster Raving Looney Party and Radio Caroline. In 1620, two men arrived outside this inn in a paper boat. John Taylor, the 'Water Poet' and Roger Bird, a vintner, took a bet they could row in such a vessel from London to Queenborough. The pair built it from brown paper on a rowing boat frame with eight large bladders to keep it afloat. They had all but sunk by the time they reached here. It is a large Victorian building overlooking the harbour and the landing place of those intrepid sailors.

RAINHAM

In AD 811, this was known Roegingaham and was the home of the Roegingas, a tribal group. There had been extensive, and ancient, trackways through and near Rainham and these were taken over by the Romans for their Watling Street. Some Roman mercenaries settled in the area and started farms after marrying local women and there is a Roman cemetery near the town.

MACKLAND ARMS

A short distance from the railway station the Mackland Arms is one of the town's best-known pubs. It is a small pub with an L-shaped bar in a terrace of early Victorian houses. It is known locally as the Office. There seems to be no historical Mackland family and the inn sign carries a gate leading to a windmill displaying a bucolic scene.

RAMSGATE

The town is an ancient fishing port that became a limb of Sandwich in association with the Cinque Ports in 1485. In 1723, according to Daniel Defoe, the inhabitants called it Roman's Gate as though the Romans had landed here. When convicts were transported to the colonies, their last point of call was here. Elizabeth Fry, prison and social reformer, died here in 1845. Mr Payne of Harbour Street owned the last sedan chair in the town and his last passenger was Lady Montefiore. The treacherous Goodwin Sands, offshore from Ramsgate, is reputed to be haunted by a Spanish galleon. It comes up the channel under full sail, onto the sands, bursts into flames and sinks into the foreshore.

ARTILLERY ARMS, WEST CLIFF ROAD

A terraced pub with leaded bow windows showing scenes of soldiers and guns from the Napoleonic Wars in France; built in 1812 at the height of those wars it was used both as an officers' mess and a brothel. It became a fully licensed pub in 1869 as the Suez Canal was opened. It has a famous name for a pub, coming from the Honourable Artillery Company that began as a guild of archers in 1537. They claim to be the oldest, and most senior, regiment of the British Army.

AUSTRALIAN ARMS, ASHBURNHAM ROAD

At one time convict ships bound for Australia and New Zealand berthed in Ramsgate's Royal Harbour and the pub was named after this event. There are very few pubs named this and the only one I know is the Australian in London and that is next door to a cricket ground where England played Australia in the first home match in 1878. The Australian Arms, Ramsgate, opened as a pub in 1849 but the flint-faced building is much older than that.

DEAL CUTTER, KINGS STREET

As, in many ports, pubs are named after local ships and boats this was after the small single-masted sailing vessel used by Revenue men when in pursuit of the smugglers. Built in 1800, at the foundation of the Royal College of Surgeons, the Deal Cutter is a typical pub of that period with one step down into the bar that means that the road has come up since building it. Opposite was once the sweetly named Rose in June pub.

EAGLE INN, HIGH STREET

A large inn named after an occasion when a member of the Tomson family of the Tomson and Wotton brewery shot an eagle as some were flying south because of the severe winter. William

Tomson shot it and took it back to the pub, which was then known as the Spread Eagle, where a replica now reigns high up on the façade. It is a large corner pub opposite the Albert Inn, on Paradise, and is well over 200 years old and was a coaching inn.

MONTEFIORE ARMS, TRINITY PLACE

A most unusual pub name; it was named after Sir Moses Montefiore, a well-known philanthropist who lived to over the age of 100. Montefiore was a campaigner for Jewish rights in the Middle East and was very much a benefactor to the poor of Ramsgate. He lived here for many years and, when he died in 1884, he was buried in a mausoleum near this pub. It is an old town pub that was once two cottages.

ROSE OF ENGLAND

Opened in 1779 at the same time that Captain Cook was murdered in the Sandwich Islands, it was once called the Rose and Crown. Behind it was a large hall called the Philharmonic Music Hall but this was destroyed by fire during a rendition of the *Fireman's Wedding*. Often Rose of England, as a pub name, now refers to the late Princess Diana as this one does.

ST LAWRENCE TAVERN

Originally called the White Horse this was 300 yards away from where it now stands. It was an eighteenth-century inn and was demolished in 1851 then moved, lock stock and all the barrels, and finally completely rebuilt and decorated, only 40 years ago. In 1817, a landlord went mad and threw himself down a well, 160 feet deep. It is said to be he who still haunts the place with his miserable mutterings and frequent outcries.

ROCHESTER

In AD 731, this was known as Hrofaescaestir, a Roman town, and, from the fourth century, known as the walled town with the bridges.

COOPER'S ARMS

Built mid-eleventh century by 1682 this was still a wattle and daub building with thatched roof and is now reputed to be the oldest pub in Kent. In 1542 the first farmer-landlord was Jonathon Quailey and it was the Cowper's Tavern, named after the sixteenth-century Coopers' Company who made wooden barrels. There is a history on a wall with a list of landlords since Quailey. There are horse brasses galore, brass measuring pots and a cooper's drawknife found in the cellar 25 years ago. It is haunted by the ghost of one of the cooper brethren who was walled up and appears every November, cowled and groaning. Behind a glass fronted cabinet is the misty image of a man with a waist-long beard and old-fashioned cloak and the landlord maintains it was it was a man who had not paid his bill. Built on the junction with Love Lane, it has views of the Norman castle and cathedral. Henry VIII met his fourth wife, Anne of Cleves, nearby and granted this tavern a coat of arms. More recently, a woman living nearby persuaded her lover to help her to kill her husband. They did so, and, as they were pushing his body into the River Medway, she got caught up in the victim's clothes, was dragged over and drowned.

Rose of England, Ramsgate

Cooper's Arms, Rochester

RUCKINGE

Hrocking in AD 786, a place of rooks owned by Hroc. Thomas Aveling, the pioneer of the steam traction engine, lived here and the smoke box door of his Aveling and Porter steamroller is on the village sign.

BLUE ANCHOR INN

In eighteenth-century slang, an 'Admiral of the Blue' was a sailor who took a pub; one who wore a blue apron. A similar expression was that he had 'hoisted the blue flag' and had become an ale-draper. Often such retired sailors gave this name to their pub and the Ruckinge inn was opened in 1738. It was once used by smugglers and, in April 1799, William Ransley, the cousin of the infamous smuggler George Ransley, became involved in a punch-up with the landlord and his wife, James and Anne Wilson. For this, he was sent to prison at Canterbury for three months. Almost a quarter of a century later, part of the Ransley Gang, James and John Hughen and Paul Pierce, were seen going into the Blue Anchor by Bow Street Runners and arrested after a struggle. They were transported to Tasmania. The Blue Anchor is a roadside inn with several bars.

RUSTHALL

RED LION

At about the time of Cade's Rebellion, when they defeated the royal troops at Sevenoaks, this inn opened its doors as an alehouse and inn for travellers and pilgrims. They claim to have the oldest licence in Kent dating to that period, 1450. The building had been in existence for many years before becoming an inn. There have been reports over the years of ghostly activity with cold spots and noises and, on one occasion, the hindquarters of a dog were seen disappearing through a bar door. Customers who have seen this animal describe it as a scruffy beast, large and curled up on the floor of the bar. There are also reports of refrigerator doors locking tight. Outside the pub is often heard the clopping sounds of a ghost described as a headless horseman, dressed in armour, and said to look like one of Cromwell's Ironsiders.

SALTWOOD

CASTLE HOTEL

This was originally three old cottages and was, for many years, a late Regency-style hotel. The original started as a hostel for the retainers and servants of the visitors to Saltwood Castle. It is a large roadside inn with a large beer garden and several bars between Sandling railway station and Hythe. There is a legend that a cottage or alehouse near here, or perhaps on the same site, was notorious as the meeting place of the four murderers of Archbishop Thomas a Beckett.

SANDGATE

CLARENDON

A super pub with sea views it is up a sharp hill from the esplanade and, on a clear day, one can see right across to France from outside the pub. Lord Clarendon was the New Warden of the Cinque Ports and decreed the small fishing village should be a seaside resort and this inn stands as his memorial. It is thought that the inn opened in 1820 as the Rose Tavern but the first real reference comes in 1871 when Henry Couchman was landlord. In 1893, there was a landslip and the whole building moved several inches leaving severe cracking. A rather wicked poltergeist has made its appearance, from time to time, throwing things out of cupboards and even microwaves ovens. According to regulars do not ask what CYCUCYFPFTIPU stands for.

SHIP INN

This interesting old pub has portraits of the regulars hanging in the bar. It backs on to the sea and is haunted by two ghosts seen in different parts of the pub. It was along this street that supplies came in for the 1st Light infantry in the eighteenth century. In 1798, the troops were based at Shornecliffe Camp when John Hogben was landlord and a popular inn it was then. The camp had been built in 1794 in preparation for the Napoleonic Wars. The Ship was also as popular during the Crimean War when the British German Legion was raised and camped nearby. In the 1920s, under the landlord Henry Beer, it was described as The World Famous Ship Inn, Sandgate. The ghosts here are the Fish Lady, who appears reeking of fish, and a soldier in Victorian uniform.

SANDWICH

In AD 710, this was Sandwicae, a sandy harbour or trading place, and became one of the original Cinque Ports. Two of the old gates survive; Barbican and Fisher Gate were built in 1384. In 1560, Elizabeth I granted permission for Flemings to live in Sandwich when escaping persecution in the Netherlands. They were accomplished market gardeners and grew the first celery in 1561. She visited the town in 1573 and stayed at the King's Lodgings for three days. The first elephant to land in England came ashore here in 1255, a present from France to Henry III for his zoo at London Tower. There is said to be hidden somewhere at Ash, Sandwich, a solid gold image of the Saxon god, Woden. In 1759, Bryan Fausee excavated the area and found a series of Saxon graves, but no sign of the gold statue. Sandwich is the last place in Kent where one can still buy huffkins. These are traditional tea breads that are thick, flat and oval with a dimple in the middle. Of course, it was the Earl of Sandwich who gave his name to that culinary delight; two pieces of bread surrounding a myriad of delectables. He had been busy playing cards and put a piece of meat in the bread; the sandwich. In the town, near the Guildhall, is No Name Street and No Name Shop.

ADMIRAL OWEN

Named after Admiral William Owen, who first served in the *Culloden*, and was then given charge of the national gunboats. He proved to be brilliant at capturing French gunboats and privateers and was, finally, promoted to Admiral. The pub was formerly the Pelican and then the Three Mariners. At a meeting between the Town Clerk and the Master of St Bartholomew's Hospital on one occasion, they spent two groats at the Pelican. The hospital was founded in 1217 as a thanksgiving for defeat by the Sandwich fleet on St Bartholomews's Day. Inside the Admiral Owen, it has bare wooden floors with open fires and chimney stacks that have been left behind by opening up the bar and with a raised dais as a restaurant. On the walls are rope knots and pictures of sailing boats, a photograph of a three-masted ship along with a model of a wherry (a river sailing boat) and pew-style seating.

Crispin Inn,
Sandwich

BELL HOTEL

King Charles I drank a glass of sack here on his way to Dover to meet Queen Henrietta Maria on her return from exile, accompanied by his brother, James (Duke of York), Prince Rupert and the Earl of Sandwich. He was presented with the spicy wine by the town mayor and drank it without dismounting from his horse. In another incident, on the same occasion, a dog bit the horse of a courtier who was dashed to the ground; apparently with foul oaths. This impressive inn on the quay was known as the Bell Tavern in the seventeenth century. In 1648, a man turned up here claiming to be the Prince of Wales and was received joyously by the Royalists of the town. His real name was Cornelius Evans and he was caught out, and languished in Canterbury Gaol for a considerable time.

CRISPIN INN

St Crispin is the patron saint of shoemakers and cobblers and is said to have paid for his travels as he spread the gospel by repairing shoes. St Crispin's Day (25 October) is the day in 1415 of the Battle of Agincourt and appears in Shakespeare's speech in Henry V. This ancient low-beamed pub is close by the old Barbican that was the toll gate for travellers over the bridge. (Near most toll gates was a 'shun gate', a small lane so that travellers could avoid paying the toll). Opened in

1491, as Columbus was preparing his exploratory fleet, the Crispin was the headquarters of the local Guild of Fishermen. It is a large corner inn with low beams and the historical date written on the outside wall. There have been reports over the years of a woman in a mobcap wandering about, but who appears to be of a happy disposition.

SARRE

This was known as Serrae in AD 761 but obscure in meaning, possibly an old name for the River Wantsum. Once, this river was a mile wide, but, by 1485, had become a narrow stream spanned by a bridge. There was a Roman fort on the river against Anglo-Saxon attacks and in 1862, a Saxon burial ground was found.

CROWN INN

Opened in the fifteenth century, the Crown is famous for cherry brandy with a secret recipe. On the front of the inn are names of people who have visited including Rudyard Kipling, Ellen Terry, Charles Dickens and Sir George Robey and it is known as the Cherry Brandy House. Built on three floors with dormer windows, it describes itself as Old Established Halfway House, Est. 1500. It is one of the rare pubs to have a priest hole from the time when Roman Catholics were hunted down. One staircase can only be entered from a bedroom that was once used to bring in smuggled goods.

SEAL

In 1086, it was known as La Sela, the sallow tree copse. Four centuries later Henry VIII acceded to the throne and married Catherine of Aragon. As a wedding present, he gave her a number of Spanish trees in the village, to remind her of home, and the trees still stand at Woodland Rise.

KENTISH YEOMAN

The name 'yeoman' has puzzled scholars for years. Some maintain it is a young man; others say it is a countryman or villager. However, the yeoman became a trusted servant; less than a squire and more than a knave and probably owned a small estate. Such farmers became the Yeomanry, a volunteer cavalry force. Therefore, the name can refer to either a soldier or farmer. This is the oldest pub in Seal and one of the oldest in Kent. It is said that the pub has been here since 1396 and is on top of an old medieval mortuary, and there is evidence of a lime pit to get rid of bodies. There is also a labyrinth of tunnels underneath (not now for public use), for people to escape whenever there was a raid by local villains. The pub has a Bat and Trap team.

FIVE BELLS

A small back street pub that was three cottages in the eighteenth century, it has a low ceiling bar decorated with photographs of the village life with a piano for singalongs. It is an eighteenth-century building on top of a fifteenth-century original. In the 1950s, it was kept by 'Ratty' Williams, who was also the local rat catcher. The first balloon ascent in England took place here in 1825. The local militia was called in to prevent the superstitious locals destroying this modern beast. Five Bells was the nautical expression for 2.30 p.m., once the traditional closing time for pubs. Opposite is Pudding Lane with a private house, Six Bells; obviously of a much superior rank to the pub.

Chequers, Sevenoaks

SEVENOAKS

The Shambles, Sevenoaks, was the old high street from Old English *scemal* for butchers and slaughterhouses. They were mainly occupied by labourers working on local estates and clustered around the old market house that was, until the nineteenth century, exactly as it was when Cade's rebellion started five centuries previously.

CHEQUERS

A one bar old timber-framed pub in a twelfth-century building that used to house the local Petty Sessions and manor courts in ancient times. There used to be a set of gallows next door to the Chequers and the guilty ones were taken from the cells near the Dorset Arms (Sevenoaks), and were dispatched shortly after their trials. These executions were watched by large crowds and one woman, looking through an upstairs window of the Chequers, saw her son being hanged and dropped dead. Since then she has been seen and heard wandering the premises with occasional cries of anguish. Some years after this event the window was blocked off from public use. The market that is now held outside the pub on Saturday mornings is from the original charter of the thirteenth century.

SHEERNESS

Known as Scerhnesse in 1203 it meant bright headland or, alternatively, from Old English *scear*, a ploughshare, referring to its geographical shape.

SHIP ON SHORE

One of the most curious follies of Kent is part of this roadside inn. A sailing ship, the *Lucky Escape*, ran aground on the beach when it was carrying a cargo of cement in barrels. They were dumped ashore and then the wet cement hardened. A local farmer knocked off the barrel staves and built this curious building. It is a roadside inn, just out of the town, that has a picture of the *Lucky Escape* on the inn sign.

TRUE BRITON

This was the name of an East Indiaman, a sailing ship of large tonnage, working the East India trade. It disappeared on its eighth trip with all hands. 'True Briton' was a nineteenth-century method of signing anonymous letters on matters of great import; rather like 'Disgusted, Tunbridge Wells', now. As a pub name, it showed patriotism by the landlord who named it. It is a large corner pub with records going back to 1828, and once there was True Briton Alley beside it. This alleyway was infamous, because one man who lived there was suspected of being Jack the Ripper. Inside the pub are many pewter pots and brassware in an L-shaped bar with a small, carved whaling boat called the 'Annabelle, Southampton 1891' on one wall. There is also, fairly rare now, a brass foot-rail along the bar.

Ship on Shore,
Sheerness

King's Arms, Shoreham

SHOREHAM

Scorham meant a homestead on a steep bank in AD 822. On a steep bank to the south of the village is a large Christian cross carved into the turf of the hill. In the church is a painting of Lt Verney Lovett Cameron, son of a former vicar. Cameron headed an expedition to Africa to find David Livingstone but met up with the bearers bringing his body back out. He carried on to be the first white man to cross Africa and later retired to write adventure books. Outside the village is the old lost hamlet of Merston, which was a stockaded Saxon settlement deserted in 1445, possibly because of a plague.

KING'S ARMS

Outside is an ostler's box for the inn servant who would attend horses as they arrived. Where this original box stood there is now a waxwork ostler looking out onto the street in Victorian-style garb. He has a large pot of ale in front of him and is flanked by the tools of his trade. The King's Arms stands on the high street near the village stream and is a large pub with an L-shaped bar.

CROWN INN

In her *Companion into Kent*, published 1934, Dorothy Gardiner tells a story from the nineteenth century. A gang of smugglers appeared at the Crown with a Spaniard who had been wounded. The daughter of Squib the Maltster, the landlord, looked after him and then married him and they lived in Shoreham. Later he was press-ganged and when he returned years later she had died and he died shortly afterwards. He is said to be the weeping man sometimes seen outside the inn. Surrounded by Georgian houses and old cottages, the Crown was built in 1454 and was once wattle and daub with a thatched roof.

OLDE GEORGE INNE

The inn is a fifteenth-century building and next door to the parish church but was built, originally, as cottages. In the early 1900s, the Rat and Sparrow Club met here and kept records of what had been slain and an annual prize was presented in April each year. To rid the countryside of pests this club would also hunt out queen wasps, jays, stoats and weasels. A painting, said to be by Samuel Palmer, is on a wall in the side bar. Occasionally they have mummers, hoodeners and other folk play groups in attendance. A handy inn for walkers and those visiting the nearby aircraft museum.

SITTINGBOURNE

This was the home town of Sir John Baker, known as Bloody Baker or the Kentish Bluebeard, who took part in the religious persecutions under Queen Mary, whom he entertained at Sissinghurst Castle, now a world famous garden.

RED LION

An ancient coaching inn on the High Street that was part of the Romans' Watling Street running between Chester and Dover. The most interesting part of the inn is the rear yard that shows what appears to be the original herringbone brickwork and gables. This may well be Elizabethan or an extremely good copy. There are red bricks laid in the courtyard and evidence of stable doors when horses were kept. Inside is a long narrow bar with brick ties on the wall and an unusual double fireplace with an aged oak beam above it. Lavatories are marked 'Squires' and 'Maidens' although it is a moot point if such accommodations were made in the fifteenth century. Henry V stayed here on his way back from Agincourt in 1415 and Henry VIII visited in 1532 as he awaited the Submission of the Clergy. As a large coaching inn, it was on the London to Canterbury run.

SMARDEN

Smeredaenne in the 1100s, a woodland pasture where butter was produced.

BELL INN

A tile-hung eighteenth-century pub from a building that went up in 1536 and was a farmhouse, a blacksmith's shop and forge before acquiring a licence in 1630. However, it was given no pub name until 1769 and these pubs were known as 'blind pigs', often run by smugglers and criminals. It used to offer extensive stabling and horse hire. Inside it is fairly rambling with stone-flagged floors and low beams. The Bell Inn is a typical Wealden building with a peg-tiled roof and a massive chimney column.

Red Lion, Sittingbourne

CHEQUERS

Over 500 years old, this is where a Napoleonic War veteran was murdered and since then there has been poltergeist activity with cutlery and crockery being moved about. One witness to an apparition saw a man standing at her bedroom with a hideous smile that dissolved away in front of her. In another case, a woman was touched on the back during the night and woke up with a mark in the shape of a cross. The Chequers is a white painted, two-storey inn with dormer windows and a bowed window on the ground floor and several bars with timber frames, and horse brasses. In the garden, it has its own duck pond.

SMARTS HILL

SPOTTED DOG

The curious name is said to have come from the three leopards of the arms of the Sidneys and was the result of a sign painter not knowing the difference between the animals the Talbot, (a hunting dog) and a leopard; however, the arms of the Sidneys are comprised of a lion and a porcupine on either side of a pheon, a broad arrow head. Now the truth has emerged: the confusion came about because the family that owned the pub for many years was the Leppards; still a well known local family. It may be that this sign was a convoluted joke on the family name. This pub was originally built at Tonbridge and floated up the river on rafts. Then it was dragged into its present position with a team of oxen in the fifteenth century. It has a peg-tiled roof with a long L-shaped bar with many prints on the walls. It is a good mile outside Penshurst. The best known of the Sidneys was Sir Phillip, who died at of wound sustained during an attack on the Spanish convoy at Zutphen, Netherlands.

SNARGATE

A twelfth-century poaching term, *Snergathe*, a gate or way where snares are set.

RED LION

Dating from 1540, when apricots were planted for the first time in Kent, this inn is known as 'Doris's' and has been in the same family, the Jemisons, since 1911. The Red Lion is set back from the road opposite the village church and has a white rendered façade with a tiled roof on two storeys. Going in, the main bar is on the left, and has, unusually for a country pub, a marble topped bar with an unusual, white, wooden, prow shaped façade. The pewter housing for the hand pumps dates from 1870 and there are still gas fitted lights. In one room is the largest collection of traditional pub games to be found in Kent. It retains many other old features including memorabilia from the early 1900s and posters from the Second World War including Jane of the *Daily Mirror* and of Churchill with bank notes on the ceiling. Outside are cycle racks and an old bicycle, quite overgrown, that might have been left by a telegram boy many years ago. The Red Lion features in the CAMRA National Inventory of pub interiors with outstanding and historic interest. Such pubs are a national treasure and should be visited before they disappear altogether under the savage tread of progress.

Spotted Dog, Smarts Hill

Red Lion, Snargate

SPELDHURST

Eighth century Speldhirst, a wooded area with wood chips. On one day each May, all roads into the village are closed for the annual pram race and fair.

GEORGE AND DRAGON

Over seven centuries old with oak beams and an original kingpost, it opened even before the Magna Carta was signed at Surrey. There are two bars and two restaurants with open fires and the largest inglenook fireplace in any Kent pub. The Village Bar has an ornate fireplace, small alcoves with pew benches, stone flags and dark panelling. Behind the vast oak front door, complete with studs and a horseshoe, is a Victorian butter churn. Legend has it that Kentish bowmen celebrated here on their return from Agincourt, 1415. (That was where the infamous V sign came from, when the French said they would have the English bowmen's fingers after the battle and the archers waved two fingers in derision when they won). On the exterior the George and Dragon is white and black beamed with a large dormer window and small framed windows.

STANFORD

DRUM INN

More than two centuries old, the Drum Inn has a military connection and was named when the Duke of Marlborough stationed his troops here to recruit local men. A drum was used to draw attention to these soldiers as they went from village to village offering the King's Shilling. The Drum was also used as a watchtower for Revenue men hunting the smugglers and other outlaws who worked in this area. The inn is white painted on two storeys with at least six dormer windows and steps leading up to the entrance. It is low beamed with bare brick pillars and plaster walls.

STAPLEHURST

The oldest church door in England hangs at this parish church. It is made in wrought iron with some Norse mythological characters. Charles Dickens was involved in a train crash just outside Staplehurst in 1865. It was derailed over the river and Dickens rescued two women and then went back to get out others. (In a letter to his friend, Mitton, Dickens described the accident and how he had to go back to his wrecked carriage to find some manuscripts he had left behind). Three Staplehurst women, who refused to attend Roman Catholic services, were burned at the sake in 1555. The vicar, Thomas Henson, reported them to Sir John Baker

Oldest church door, Staplehurst

(Bloody Baker) who had them tried. In 1763, John Wesley preached at Staplehurst and was arrested along with the house owner and fourteen other people. Charged under an Act of 1664 the case had to be dismissed when the Magistrate was advised that it had been repealed 70 years previously.

THREE HORSESHOES

There is a history of landlords here going back to when it opened in 1690. Built of brick and weatherboarding there is a walnut tree in the garden dating back to 1590. Old books are available for quiet drinkers. Many country pubs are called the Three Horseshoes on the joke that a horse on the way to the blacksmiths would only have three shoes and the farmer would have to wait in the pub until it was shod. It was, in fact, after the Worshipful Company of Farriers (1673) and to the Ferrers family, earls of Derby.

KING'S HEAD

This is a huge and most attractive corner pub opposite the parish church with hung red tiles and a number of bars. There are two gravestones in the garden and, when one was removed, there was serious haunting in the pub consisting of heavy mists and weird sounds. Domestic pets stay away from several parts of the inn and garden

King's Head, Staplehurst

STELLING MINNISS

GEORGE INN

Late at night, when all is still, the muffled hoof-beats of a gang of knights are heard going past this inn, which is four centuries old. They say it is those knights who galloped through in 1170 after slaying Thomas a Becket at Canterbury at the apparent behest of Henry II. The king is alleged to have said, 'What a parcel of fools and dastards have I nourished in my house that not one of them will avenge me of one upstart clerk.' The four knights took him at his word and avenged him at the altar steps of Canterbury Cathedral. There is also a pub indwell dressed in eighteenth-century costume alongside the apparition of a black dog.

STROOD

Strod in AD 889, a marshy area overgrown with brushwood.

CRISPIN AND CRISPIANUS

This inn was once a meeting place for the cobblers and shoemakers in the district and the inn sign carries portraits of the two brothers. The pair are saints who had evangelised Gaul and southern Britain in the third century and were martyred by Emperor Maximus Herculeus in AD 286. They were cobblers and shoemakers who had lived in various parts of Kent. It is a roadside inn on three storeys, white painted woodwork with white brick; the first floor overhangs the pavement and there are dormer windows. It is a basic two bar inn with a collection of books in the snug.

THREE CRUTCHES, OLD WATLING STREET

Almost six centuries old, this weatherboarded and slate roof pub overlooks a great vista from the rear beer garden. The inn sign shows Crutched Friars who were distinguished by one cross on their backs. The word is a corruption from the Crossed Friars who were of the Holy Cross order. They wore a red cross on their habit and carried a silver cross before them. The word crutch comes from the Latin root *crux*. The crutch was used by people who were crippled but there is no truth that the Crutched Friars were all crippled. The pub has two main bars, a large dining room and lounge area. The pub was at one time called the Three Crosses and then changed to Three Crouches. However, a more recent landlord decided to change this to the Three Crutches, pronounced crooches. At least three ghosts haunt this pub. The landlady told me that she and a large number of staff and local regulars have seen a man wander through the public bar and the dining room. 'But it seems quite a harmless old ghost.' she said.

SUTTON VALLENCE

Cricketer John Willes has a memorial in the church here. He was the man who introduced round-arm bowling to cricket after copying his sister, Christina, who could not bowl under arm because her hoop skirts were caught up with her arm when she practised it. Willes lived at Bellingham House in the village and was cricket coach to Alfred Mynn, the Lion of Kent.

Three Crutches, Strood

SWAN INN

Built in 1467 with two bars and a separate restaurant there are bay windows and an overhanging gallery with a massive peg-tiled roof. The pavement is higher than the road for easy horse mounting. There is a lease dating back to 1467 but parts of it are twelfth century. This has been a popular inn sign since the fourteenth century and was favoured in the coats of arms of Henry VIII and Edward III. Edward swore 'The vow of the Swan' that he would wreak vengeance on the Scots for their violent ways. The Swan is surrounded by many very old houses.

TENTERDEN

Tentwardene in 1179, a woodland pasture of the Thanet people. Benjamin Franklin, famous American scientist, lived nearby and worshipped at a Unitarian chapel when he was working locally in the printing trade. He had been sent to this country to buy fonts and other printing equipment and then left to his own devices without income. The wide street of the town shows it was used as a market town for sheep and a turning place for coaches that need a large area. In the Middle Ages it was an important market town and there are Tudor, Georgian and Victorian houses along the street.

WHITE LION

This inn name is usually after the heraldic device of Edward IV, the earls of March or the dukes of Norfolk. It is a sixteenth-century coaching inn with an elegant frontage with pillared porch, bowed and dormer windows, and a side entrance for coaches. It was built facing a wide tree-lined street that includes many historic buildings and inside the White Lion are aged beams, inglenook fireplaces and much local memorabilia.

WILLIAM CAXTON

Formerly called the Black Horse it was a smugglers' inn from the sixteenth century. Known as the Father of English printing, Caxton learned of the printing system in Germany and brought it back to England. The first book to be published by this method in England was, of course, the Holy Bible, in 1475. The first book to be published in the English language was by Caxton at Bruges entitled *Recuyell of the Histories of Troye* in the same year. It is a low-beamed pub with a large open fire and paper money pinned to the old oak beams.

WOOLPACK

The old mayor's parlour and magistrates' court were both here in this red tiled inn. But, in the meantime, smugglers were using a back room for their trading. When a new floor was constructed some years ago at the Woolpack, a pipe was found connected to a cask below in which brandy was hidden if the revenue men appeared. The pub name refers to the business that brought so much prosperity to this part of Kent.

Swann Inn, Sutton Vallence

TEYNHAM

In AD 789, this was Teneham, the homestead of Tena. During the reign of Henry VIII Richard Harris planted an orchard of sweet cherry and apple trees. He had brought these from France when he heard of Henry's appetite for the fruits.

FOX

The inn is surrounded by nineteenth-century cottages and an oast house at the end of the village. It is a large corner pub re-built in the early 1900s on a much older site. In the Middle Ages, it was said the fox was in league with the devil and a single bite would kill a person. There was also a country story that on any day, when rain and sun appear together, is the time when foxes get married.

SWAN

An old coaching inn that was rebuilt after a fire in the Tudorbethan style with heavy gables and white paint. It stands on the high street but several yards back from its original position. The swan, as an inn name, has been around since the fourteenth century as it featured on many coats of arms. There is a legend that swans never sing during their lives but, as they are about to die, make a melodic sound; this is the last thing they do: hence, swansong.

GEORGE INN

A high street pub going back four centuries, this one has a sloping ceiling with old beams. It is haunted by two old people chatting in what used to be the snug. One customer who heard them reported that the conversation ended as the back door closed on them going out. There are some old photographs of the pub and a picture of the village fire handcart, still being used in 1916. The windows are etched with the Rigden Brewery advertisment that went many years ago.

TONBRIDGE

Known as Tonebrige in 1086 it was, probably, a bridge belonging to the estate or manor.

IVY HOUSE, HIGH STREET

Opened at the time of Edward IV in the late 1400s this was once a horse keeper's house. It was known as the Elephant and Castle and the inn sign still shows this. Because it was covered in ivy locals referred to it as the Ivy House and the name has stuck. Inside it is delightful with open log fire, church pews with numbers on so the pew-renters knew where they were to sit, leaning oak beams and a salmon caught locally weighing 23lb. One of those pubs worth visiting before it feels the heavy hand of progress and renovation. A sign from 1868 reads that 'Poachers will be shot' from the nearby Somerhill Estate.

MAN OF KENT, EAST STREET

The inn sign here now features a man working in the fields rather than an earlier one of Field Marshall French, a Kent man of the First World War. In Victorian times, local labourers took what they called a 'snob day' and went drinking instead of working. What is good enough for them is good enough for us was their attitude. Over these rebellious drinking sessions at this inn, the landlord, Tom Cheal, presided when it opened at 6 a.m. Ale was served in blue earthenware jugs at four-pence a quart and his wife made sure they had a mid-day meal. In those days

Ivy House, Tonbridge

the bar floor was covered with sawdust. The Man of Kent is a long building with cream and black painted frontage and weatherboarding surrounded by early nineteenth-century cottages. Inside it is low beamed with several bars and, over the open fire, is an agricultural implement like a large yoke. Part of the walls have been stripped away to reveal the old timber framing to create partitions.

ROSE AND CROWN, HIGH STREET

A noble looking eighteenth-century posting and coaching inn with a fine pillared portico, the Rose and Crown opens onto the High Street. Earliest records show it in 1625 and in 1695 an indenture refers to the Roase and Crown. An early nineteenth-century Duchess of Kent stayed here with her sister, Princess Victoria, the then future queen. Inside are old beams and Jacobean panelling. At the side of the inn is the old coach entrance to the stables. In 1893, the landlord was Tom Pawlett, who played cricket for Kent.

Beau Nash, Tunbridge Wells

STAG'S HEAD, STAFFORD ROAD

Behind the castle is this grade II listed building which dates back to 1756 as a pub. Once it had its own brewery on the premises. A stag's head was kept on walls at many old houses as a symbol of virility, wisdom and life. Once there was a large notice at this inn that read: 'Rules of this Tavern. Four pence a night for Bed; Sixpence with supper; No more than five to sleep in one bed; No boots to be worn in Bed; Organ grinders to sleep in the Wash house; No dogs allowed upstairs; No beer allowed in the kitchen; No Razor Grinders or Tinkers taken in.'

YE OLDE CHEQUERS INN

On the inn sign is a macabre reminder of summary justice, a hangman's noose. One of the men hanged outside this pub was Wat Tyler's brother after the failed Peasant's Revolt of 1381. Originally built in 1270 a lot of it is now sixteenth century with original timbers. It is a low-beamed L-shaped bar with brasses and an old yard of ale glass. Many pubs named this were after the money changers' board and who held their business here. The courtyard is said to be haunted by two men duelling with swords and the inn features in novels by Jeffrey Farnol. Just outside is a Victorian horse water trough filled with flowers.

TROTTISCLIFFE

Pronounced 'Trosley' the land was given to the See of Rochester by Offa, King of Mercia, in AD 788. It was then known as Trottes clyva, the cliff or hill of a Saxon, Trott.

GEORGE

There are still oast houses around this inn that became an alehouse in 1782 and fully licensed in 1831. The building is 500 years old and, in 1980, the chimney came crashing down into the inglenook fire. In the dust and rubble were found shoes, a leather purse and clay pipes that had been walled in over a century previously. Inside are timbered bars with cosy alcoves and an inglenook fireplace.

TUNBRIDGE WELLS

In 1606, Lord North was riding home to London and came across a spring of cool, iron, flavoured water. He took a sample home and had it analysed and reports maintained it was good for health. By 1620, it was a summer resort for aristocrats and in 1630, Queen Henrietta Maria went to recover after the birth of the future Charles II. In 1632 Dr. Lodwick Rowzee recommended drinking 15 pints a day of the Tunbridge Water.

BEAU NASH, MOUNT EPHRAIM

An old pub with leaded windows in a courtyard off the common, it was named after the dandy, Richard Beau Nash, of the eighteenth century. Nash went to live in Tunbridge Wells in 1735 and established himself as Master of Ceremonies and insisted on certain codes of behaviour and organised gambling for gentlemen. Although Nash lived by gambling, he died penniless in 1745. The inn, once known as the Mount Ephraim Hotel and then the Hare and Hounds, has old, bare, wooden boards with upright iron pillars and mullioned windows. It is a grade II listed building and found down a long drive and outside is a splendid tree shaded beer garden.

UPPER UPNOR

TUDOR ROSE

For many years, this was the King's Head but changed to avoid confusion with another King's Head nearby. Tudor was from the Welsh name, Tewdyr. Owain Tudor married Catherine the widow of Henry V and his grandson, Henry VII, was the first Tudor king. The Tudor rose was adopted as a badge by Henry VII and combined the red and white roses of Yorkshire and Lancashire. Below Upnor Castle, in a cobbled street, the Tudor Rose overlooks the River Medway and the old Chatham Dockyard and there is a seventeenth-century wall in part of the garden. There are several bars and two old cooking ranges inside.

North Pole, Wateringbury

WATERINGBURY

Over the parish church door is a dumb borsholder, a Saxon piece from the Court Moot. This instrument has a spike at one end to smash down the doors of criminals when in hot pursuit. It is a three feet five inches long staff built of wood with metal rings. Originally, it was a badge of office of the elder appointed to attend the meetings of the Hundred Council. Each man was elected for one year and was paid a penny a year by each resident. The last person to hold it was Thomas Clampard, who died in 1748. In the village, there is also the village lockup that is now a grade II listed building and was last used in 1842.

NORTH POLE

This pub name first appeared in London in the 1860s, many years before the North Pole was reached by Robert Edward Peary in 1909. The first sign at this inn was a simple wooden pole nicknamed the North Pole. Actually, to get to this pub is rather like trying to get to the North Pole proper. Walking or cycling from the village centre it is about one and half miles and uphill all the way. It is probably about 300 years old and was a coaching inn on a main run and the stables, now houses, were next door. Once it was known as the North Toll, because this was where the toll money was collected from coaches and other horse traffic. Part of the inn shows the original interior timber framing as a feature and there are a large number of paintings by Frank Oakley, a local artist. Mr Oakley, a retired headmaster born in 1914, was also church organist. In 1920, one landlord, F.G. Cronk, penned an ode to the North Pole that is now on a wall near the entrance. It is said to be haunted by a man called Mr Walterstone who wanders around chattering and tapping people on the shoulders.

WELL HILL

KENT HOUNDS

There are over 3,000 key fobs hanging from the ceiling and a doodlebug in a glass case at this village local. The building is over four centuries old and there has been an inn here for at least 250 years. There is an aviary in the garden and it is a popular pub with walkers and cyclists. (There is one pub actually called the Fob Watch in the midlands where there is an inn sign of a large fob watch outside to remind passers by that this was once the centre of watchmakers. The fob was a small pocket for watch or cash that may have come from a German word).

WESTERHAM

The village name is from the Saxon for westerly home. Westerham church has rare fourteenth-century octagonal tower steps. There is a General Wolfe memorial by Sir Edward Burne-Jones on the green opposite the pub.

GRASSHOPPER ON THE GREEN

Named after the heraldic arms of Sir Thomas Gresham (1519-79), the English merchant and financier who lived nearby, the inn overlooks the green and Sir Winston Churchill's statue. (At Cambridge the name 'grasshopper' refers to the university lawn tennis club). John Frith, a famous Protestant martyr, was the son of a former landlord who was burned at the stake in 1553. The pub was centuries old, even then. Coaches, mail and passenger, ran between here and Fleet Street and the next stop was the Bell at Bromley. There is much reference to Sir Winston Churchill in the pub; a poster on the door reads, 'Let us go forward together'. There are small leaded pane windows, several small bars and a collection of small milk jugs and brasses.

GENERAL WOLFE

James Wolfe was born in this village in 1727 and joined the army aged only 14. Promoted to Major General, he went on to become Wolfe of Quebec. He took on General Montcalm on the Heights of Abraham where both were killed in 1759. He lived at what is now Quebec House, and part of it is given over to a museum with family portraits and memorabilia. Set at the eastern end of the town, the General Wolfe is a weatherboarded inn with three bars leading from each other. The main bar it is cream painted wood panels with dark wooden panels below. There is a log fire and small windows and it is well beamed. (A note reads 'Duck or grouse'.) It is a classic Kent inn over three centuries old, with some parts even older, and has a long narrow bar with an alcove and horses brasses. Opposite the pub is the Millennium 2000 garden and pond that was ceded as land to the Manor of Squerrye in 1775, but now run by the people of Westerham.

Kent Hounds, Well Hill

Grasshopper, Westerham

General Wolfe, Westerham

GEORGE AND DRAGON

General Wolfe stayed here on his last night in England before leaving for Canada and Quebec. Built in the seventeenth century it is a traditional coaching inn with oak beams and is a fine building with dormer windows and an unusual entrance porch. There is a large open plan bar with beamed ceilings and walls hung with tankards and brassware. There is also an overhanging balcony from two rooms. Viewed from outside there is a nice collection of old lamps on windowsills that must have been welcoming to pilgrims and travellers coming in off the old Pilgrims' Way.

WEST FARLEIGH

TICKLED TROUT

A Victorian inn that was named after the trout stream nearby coming off the Great Stour. It has a timber frame that indicates it was built on much older premises going back to the mid 1600s. The Tickled Trout is decorated with fishing nets and unusual knots in rope and an angler painted on the outside. Poaching fishermen would slip a hand under rocks and gently move a hand along the fish until it was hypnotised and then suddenly whip it out onto the bank; hence tickled trout. This is what appears on this wall mural. It is a long white building with a huge beer garden off the road. The inn sign shows a giggling trout with just one finger underneath its belly. The mural on the wall shows a kingfisher bird watching with more than a degree of interest.

George and the Dragon,
Westerham

WEST HYTHE

BOTOLPH'S BRIDGE INN

A rather plain and modernised building set in the marshes and named after St Botolph who lived in the seventh century. The inn sign shows his body being carried over a river with a shaft of light coming from Heaven. It stands on the junction of five marsh lanes near the Royal Military Canal built in 1805 against French invasions. The little that is known about him comes from the writings of Folcard, a monk in the eleventh century. Most of Botolph's work was connected with the east midlands and the north of England. His name is perpetuated in Boston, Lincolnshire and Boston, Massachusetts. This comes from Botulestan, 1130, stone of a man called Botwulf.

WEST PECKHAM

In 1997, some thieves stole 12 wooden statues from the church and the vicar publicly stated they should have their hands chopped off. The resultant publicity ensured their return by a north London antique dealer who had bought them.

SWAN ON THE GREEN

A two bar inn overlooking the village green and close to the parish church, the building is over five centuries old and has been licensed since 1685, the year of Judge Jeffreys and the Bloody Assizes when 320 rebels were executed. The pub name Swan has been a popular one since the fourteenth century and refers to the bird itself or the much favoured insignia of Henry VIII and Edward III on which it featured. All the beams and brickwork have been exposed with a bare wood floor and log fires. The inn carries its own microbrewery making Black Swan stout; a *rara avis*, indeed

WESTWELL

WHEEL INN

Off the beaten track, the Wheel has survived here for over 250 years as an inn, and was an alehouse before that. It is named after the wheel on which St Catherine was martyred in the third century. (Now she is the patroness of young women and one of the fourteen Holy Helpers in Heaven). On the inn sign, it is clear that not all the spokes are the same. In the Second World War, some New Zealanders, stationed nearby, said they had spent enough money in the pub to have bought some spokes: two of the spokes were then painted in the Kiwi colours. There are three connecting rooms with tiled floors and collections of teapots and old photographs. Just two miles away is Hothfield Common that is now a nature reserve with mosses, dragonflies, orchids and other fauna and flora.

WHITSTABLE

Witestaple in 1086, a white post or the post of a councillor. One Whitstable man, a deep-sea diver, located a wrecked ship from the Armada off the coat of Galway. With the proceeds he built a row of houses called Dollar Row on the Island Wall at Whitstable. Just outside the railway station is a cycle track named the Crab and Winkle Way.

BEAR AND KEY

In 1850, gas lighting came to Whitstable and 1,000 people met here to celebrate at the inn. It is a four-storey building and got its name from a corruption of Baron's Key, an adjacent road. On the inside walls are advertisements for horse and coach trips starting at one shilling and sixpence (seven and a half new pence).

SHIP CENTURION, ARMINIUS

A large three-storey inn from the mid-Victorian era, it was built on earlier premises. An unusual and confusing name as it refers to two different pieces of history. The ship referred to the is the vessel in which George, Lord Anson (1697-1762) made a round-the-world trip between 1740 and 1744. He wrote a book about this trip, published in 1748, but still available today called *Voyage around the World*. He also won many sea battles and rose to be First Lord of the Admiralty. Where pubs have been named this, they have also usually carried a Roman centurion on the inn sign. In this case it is Arminius, a German chieftain of the Cherusci tribe who had been an officer in the Roman Legions. In AD 9, he destroyed an invading Roman force commanded by Quintilius Varus and saved Germany from becoming a Roman province, but was treacherously murdered by a member of his own family in AD 19.

Centurion Ship, Whitstable

WICKHAMBREAUX

Wicham in AD 948, and Wykham Breuhuse by 1270, from the de Brayhuse family.

HOODEN HORSE

There was a custom of 'hoodening' in Kent and in 1859, a German and his wife were spending Christmas at Lower Hardres. The woman was an invalid and was wheeled out to see the hoodener's entertainment at this inn when the 'horse' pretended to jump at her snapping the jaws viciously. The terrified woman sprang out of her chair, ran away and was able to walk again. This village centre pub is named after the hoodner and his horse.

ROSE INN

The rose is the emblem of silence and since 1526 has been the sign over the church confessional; it also refers to the term, *sub rosa*, under the rule of silence. This Rose Inn dates back to 1302 just after the first Prince of Wales was created and recorded as a farmhouse in the Domesday Book of 1086.

WINGHAM

Uuigincggaham in AD 834 homestead of Wiga or, possibly, heathen temple. The first elephant to land at England came through Wingham in 1255. It stopped when it saw a bull and the enraged bull charged it. The elephant, using tusk and trunk, tossed the bull some yards and killed it. It is a picturesque village with the Old Watchmaker's Cottage opposite Sweet Love Place. The village has a tree lined high street and ancient houses. Wingham was once an important place, both socially and ecclesiastically, and was granted a market licence by Henry III.

RED LION

Over 70 years ago the inn was described as having a projecting storey with high pitched roof and moss-clad tiles and no dormer windows 'to break its sky line'. It then had the old Sessions Room with thirteenth-century architecture and was last used as a courtroom in the late 1800s. The writer praised the transom windows with mullions and hoped (at the time) they would never be taken over by restorers. To present they have not been, so it looks very much the same as it did. Outside is a Victoria Regina post box set into the wall.

WITTERSHAM

Wihtriceshamme in 1032, promontory of Wihtric.

SWAN INN

In the same year that Bunyan published *Pilgrim's Progress* in 1672 this inn opened its doors to drovers and other travellers. However, more formal records give this as 1684. For some years, it was open plan but has now reverted to two bars. Each year they stage a conker championship. Once it was a cottage and an alehouse and now the two bars are fed from a central bar counter and restaurant. Recently it has had all the old rendering taken away to reveal the original brickwork. With due regard for their county hero, the Swan now sells Wat Tyler bitter beer.

WOODCHURCH

BONNY CRAVAT

This is the local pronunciation of the *bonne crevette*, a good prawn. It was possibly a corruption of the name of a French fishing or smuggling boat that used to operate along the coast, *La Bonne Curvette*. On the other hand, it could have been named after the yew tree fence that surrounded the pub, known as a carvet, but now replaced with box hedge. It is a large cream painted and green-shuttered building opposite the parish church and is at the side of a lane leading down to a very fine mill.

SIX BELLS

Many old pubs in Kent have opened up their premises from three or four bars into one large bar, usually with a restaurant. In doing so they have exposed the timber framing and, for the most part, kept this as a feature separating different rooms. It has been successfully used at this Six Bells. Another feature here is the weighty wisteria tree that is supported in front of the pub by a specially built trellis. As it is a listed tree, it cannot be cut down although it causes some

Six Bells, Woodchurch

problems with the tiles. Just down the road, on the village green, is the old parish-pump dated 1878, from which most residents would have drawn their water.

WOODNESBOROUGH

A village with a long street that was known as Wanesberge in 1086 and Wodnesbeorge by 1100. This was from the Saxon for a mound or hill associated with the heathen god, Woden. The church of St Mary the Virgin stands on a hill outside the village and it is thought that the site was an ancient religious one, even before the Saxons arrived. There has been legend throughout Kent that a golden statue of the Woden was buried hereabouts.

CHARITY INN

A most unusual name for a pub in the centre of the village, the Charity Inn has a number of bars including Private and Public. It is built on two storeys with a steeply pitched roof and etched glass windows indicating it was a Fremlin's pub. For a short time, it was known as the Poacher but then reverted to the Charity Inn. Many years ago, local farmers employed people and gave them tokens for food and drink here. This was kept in a slotted wooden box and, at the end of the week, the farmer collected these tokens and exchanged them for money when he sold his fruit and vegetables, and then paid back the landlord. There is a list of landlords going back to 1719 when the first was Richard Sanders. It appears to have been called the Charity Inn since 1734. At one time, there were five pubs in this small village. The old inn sign shows a young girl but the present one is somewhat enigmatic, in that it seems to include the fish of the early Christian's secret signs.

WORMSHILL

Godselle in 1086 and Wotnesell by 1225, the hill of the heathen god Woden or, perhaps, a shelter for swine.

RINGLESTONE INN

Opened in 1553 as Lady Jane Grey was proclaimed Queen, who reigned but a short time, it was originally a hospice for monks and became an alehouse in 1615. It still has the original brick and flint walls, oak beams and inglenook fireplaces with much old English furniture. It features one magnificent seventeenth-century dresser with the exhortation 'A Ryght Joyeuse and Welcome greeting to Ye all' carved into it. This exhortation also appears on the inn sign. In one reception room is an old oak monastery table. Once it was owned by two women who practised shooting their guns through the windows and opened and closed the pub as they felt like. Legend has it that when they felt like closing up for the night one would appear with a gun and invite people to go home. When the dining room was added, the tables were made from the timbers of an eighteenth century Thames barge. Across the road is a tree-shaded beer garden and, at the rear, are four ponds linked by waterfalls. The Ringlestone is said to be haunted by a previous landlord.

Charity Inn, Woodnesborough

WORTH

The name meant an enclosed settlement in the twelfth century. It was reported that Archbishop Thomas a Beckett fled from Worth Creek, rather than Sandwich, where the king's spies would have spotted him. One tall tale tells of Henry V landing here from St Crispin's Day battle at Agincourt and meeting an alewife in the village. They are reported to have lived together for some time at a Worth inn that has been known as the St Crispin Inn ever since. (Although it is also said that it was one of his courtiers who fell for the woman, and that seems more likely). Between the church and the Crispin Inn is a pond and duck house behind the war memorial.

ST CRISPIN INN

This man is the patron saint of cobblers and shoemakers and his day is 25 October, the day of the Battle of Agincourt in 1415. As he spread the gospel throughout Kent, he made and repaired shoes for a living. There are a number of pubs named after St Crispin and his brother, Crispianus, throughout Kent. This Crispin is a great old inn with the date 1690 above the door and once the haunt of smugglers. It is surrounded by seventeenth and eighteenth-century houses. The Crispin is a long white building with two storeys and dormer windows in the steep, tiled roof. Inside it has a series of rooms, all being served from a large open plan bar. The pub has a Bat and Trap team

WROTHAM

Uurotaham in AD 788 this was the homestead of Wrota. In 1536, Henry VIII was staying at Wrotham when he heard of the death of Anne Boleyn. The church of St George, Wrotham, is thought to have been the first dedicated to that saint in England.

BULL HOTEL

One man, called Old Sobers, was the son of a smuggler in the nineteenth century. He left writings about his trade and at the age of 17 took a cartload of brooms to sell in London and came back home with £1,000. (This had come from silk, lace, tobacco and brandy that had been hidden beneath the brooms). In 1794, Lt-Col. Shadwell was shot dead by a smuggling gang outside this inn. Two were caught by the soldiers and beaten to death outside and there is a stone recording this event.

YALDING

Hallinges in 1086 and Ealding by 1207, the village of Ealda. In the village is an ancient lock-up for the local criminals. The 450 feet long bridge over the river was constructed in the 1400s on the site of a previous wooden bridge and is the longest surviving medieval bridge in Kent. At the parish church of St Peter and St Paul is a weathervane dating back to 1734. Iron railings for St Paul's Cathedral, London, were loaded onto barges at Yalding.

ANCHOR INN

An ancient inn that was probably the home of a water bailiff and the only one left that is still thatched throughout Kent as far as can be ascertained. It is not surprising it is called the Anchor as it is built on the Rivers Medway, Teise and Beult. The Anchor was owned by the Upper Medway Navigation Company until they sold it in 1871 for £350 and went bankrupt in 1910. (This was apt,

Anchor Inn, Yalding

because at that time to 'swallow the anchor' meant to go bankrupt). A church cycling club started here in 1922 after they had been banned from cycling on Sundays. They met at the Anchor and tried to choose a name for the club and one, a soldier returned from France said, 'Ca ne fait rien'; 'It does not matter', and it became the San Fairy Ann Club, as it is today. The tiny snug is entered by a door only four feet high and has ancient beams in a very low room. There are two inglenook fireplaces and, from one ceiling hang, hundreds of small jugs and mugs.

WALNUT TREE

A fifteenth-century inn with inglenook fireplace and original beams and hung with local hops. Outside it is a white painted pub with vast beams and brick and dormer windows in a high-pitched roof. Yalding is at the junction of three rivers crossed by an ancient narrow stone bridge. Sometimes this pub name is the Bannut Tree in Kent. In this case, it is decorated with hops, hop-sacks and pictures of the days when labourers picked hops by hand. Small paned windows reveal a large number of blue bottles arrayed along the shelves.

Other local titles published by Tempus

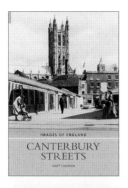

Canterbury Streets
JANET CAMERON

Fine craftsmen from medieval times to the Tudors and Stuarts have left their mark on Canterbury's streets amd thoroughfares, from pilgrim inns and medieval timber-framed houses to the striking Norman cathedral in the city centre. Take a tour around the streets of Canterbury and discover the history of the streets, the people and the places contained within them. *Canterbury Streets* will surely delight all those who know the area as it was and those who live in the city today.

0 7524 3398 9

Folklore of Kent
FRAN AND GEOFF DOEL

This fascinating book explores the folklore, legends, customs and songs of Kent, and the causative factors underlying them. From saints to smugglers, hop-pickers to hoodeners, mummers to May garlands, wife sales to witchcraft, this book charts the traditional culture of this populous and culturally significant southern county.

0 7524 2628 1

Haunted Kent
JANET CAMERON

Haunted Kent contains spooky stories from around the county, including the hunchbacked monk at Boughton Malherbe, the black dog of Leeds and the well-known tale of Lady Blanche of Rochester Castle. This fascinating collection of strange sightings and happenings in the county's streets, churches, public houses and country lanes is sure to appeal to anyone wanting to know why Kent is known as the most haunted county in England.

0 7524 3605 8

Voices of Kent and East Essex Hop Pickers
HILARY HEFFERNAN

Right up to the late 1950s, the annual hop-picking season provided a welcome escape for thousands of families who lived and worked in the poorer parts of London, who would migrate every year to the hop gardens of Kent and Sussex to pick the harvest. The photographs and reminiscences in this book tell a fascinating story; of hardship, adventures, mishaps, misfortune and laughter experienced during hardworking holidays among the bines.

0 7524 3240 0

If you are interested in purchasing other books published by Tempus, or in case you have difficulty finding any Tempus books in your local bookshop, you can also place orders directly through our website

www.tempus-publishing.com